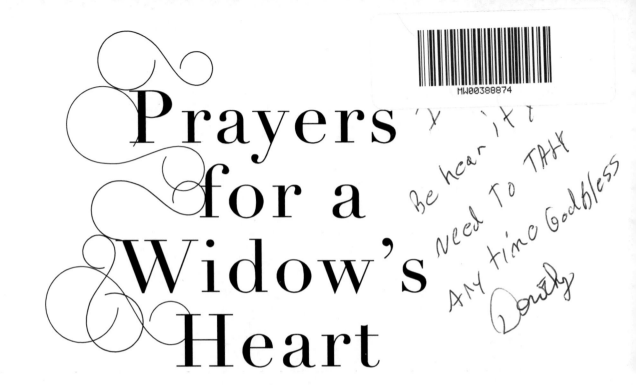

Prayers for a Widow's Heart

Honest Conversations with God

MARGARET NYMAN

Discovery House.
from Our Daily Bread Ministries

Prayers for a Widow's Heart:
Honest Conversations with God

Discovery House is affiliated with Our Daily Bread Ministries, Grand Rapids, Michigan.

Requests for permission to quote from this book should be directed to: Permissions Department, Discovery House, P.O. Box 3566, Grand Rapids, MI 49501, or contact us by e-mail at permissionsdept@dhp.org.

All Scripture quotations, unless otherwise indicated, are taken from the Holy Bible, New International Version®, NIV®. Copyright © 1973, 1978, 1984, 2011 by Biblica, Inc.™ Used by permission of Zondervan. All rights reserved worldwide. www.zondervan.com. The "NIV" and "New International Version" are trademarks registered in the United States Patent and Trademark Office by Biblica, Inc.™

Nyman, Margaret.
    Prayers for a widow's heart : honest conversations with God / Margaret Nyman.
        pages cm
    ISBN 978-1-62707-357-8
1. Widows—Prayers and devotions. I. Title.
    BV4908.N965 2015
    242'.4--dc23

Interior design by Melissa Elenbaas

Printed in the United States of America

First printing in 2015

To my sister Mary,

the most Christlike woman I know

and my dearest friend.

CONTENTS

INTRODUCTION

IF YOU ARE A WIDOW, this book was written with you in mind. I too am a widow, which means you and I probably think alike as we sort through our daily concerns.

Many of us have a deep, overwhelming longing to have our husbands back. Never mind that we know it can't actually happen; it doesn't stop us from wanting it. True, life will never be the same without our mates—but if you're willing to trust your worry and pain to God and His good plans for you, life can indeed become good again. Different, certainly, but good.

Maybe you're angry at God for letting your husband die and have no desire to adjust to widowhood. It might feel better pondering the what-if's and if-only's of your past. If so, the prayers that follow can help. It isn't because of what I've written but because of the One to whom the prayers are addressed. Our God knows exactly how you're feeling. And He has the ability to make you whole again.

Maybe your thoughts are ambivalent toward Him. You're not sure you want to engage with Him at all. Please know that, no matter what you're feeling, His love for you is fervent and unshakeable. Whether you sense it or not, God is tenderly watching over you, gently tugging you toward a future He has custom designed just for you. And He longs to talk to you about it.

And if you ever find yourself in a confusing place, unable to decide where to go next, your best move will always be toward God. He is never without an ample supply of encouragement and hope, or a fresh way to tackle your every problem. God has shown that to me—which is why I know He'll come through for you.

You might want to use these short, topical prayers to sort through your distress. If you do, you'll find God will gradually bring order to your jumbled thoughts. Call out to Him any time, day or night, knowing He is ever eager for one-on-one time with you.

Margaret

"This is what the LORD says . . .

'Call to me and I will answer you and tell you

great and unsearchable things you do not know.'"

Jeremiah 33:2–3

PART 1

SORROWING
with Hope

HEART TO HEART

The word of God . . .

is a discerner of the thoughts and intents of the heart.

Hebrews 4:12 (KJV)

DEAR FATHER,

THE MORE I GET TO KNOW YOU, the more I see you are an all-or-nothing God. Your followers—and I'm one of them—are either all-in or not in at all. Even those who seem to have one foot in heaven and one in the world are really in one or the other. And you know who's who.

That's because you can look inside people and see their true motives and desires. You know what your children are thinking, and you never experience an error in judgment. Such accuracy is both reassuring and unsettling.

When you look into my heart, what do you see? I hope it's that my motives and desires line up with your directives, Lord. My problem isn't in knowing *what* to do as much as knowing *how* to do it while I stumble through widowhood. How can I be all-in with you and your will for me, when I'm really wishing I was living a different life? That sounds like I'm not in at all.

Right now I'm struggling to get used to my husband's absence. Your scriptural instruction is to be thankful in all circumstances and to "rejoice always." If I was all-in with you, wouldn't I feel thankful and joyful? How can I be thankful for grief and joyful about widowhood?

> "The LORD searches every heart
>
> and understands every desire and every thought.
>
> If you seek him, he will be found by you."
>
> 1 Chronicles 28:9

Though sometimes it's disturbing to realize you look directly into my heart, I also take comfort in it. I hope you've seen there how much I love you and how badly I want to please you. I do want to be thankful and rejoice, as you say. But some days I'm just not up to it.

I know you want me to be an all-in daughter. But losing my husband was a tremendous knockdown, and I'm having trouble getting back on my feet. I want you to know, though, that I'm listening for your voice. I may not be consistently thanking you and rejoicing, but I like to think that one day in the not-too-distant future, you'll show me how—right in the middle of my widowhood.

I love you, Father, and I know you are loving me back, even during this time that I struggle to be all-in. And when I think of that, I'm suddenly thankful . . . maybe even to the point of rejoicing? Not about widowhood, but about your loving, heart-to-heart presence during these painful days. I appreciate you more than I'm able to show you.

And maybe, in spite of everything, that means I'm really all-in with you.

In the name of Jesus I pray. Amen.

The purpose of my instruction is that

all believers would be filled with love that comes from

a pure heart, a clear conscience, and genuine faith.

1 Timothy 1:5 (NLT)

HUNGER PAINS

The lions may grow weak and hungry,

but those who seek the LORD lack no good thing.

Psalm 34:10

DEAR FATHER,

THESE DAYS I'M EXPERIENCING an intense hunger to talk to my husband. No matter what was going on in our lives as individuals, we always found time to talk things over. I miss that terribly.

If I was bothered by something a friend said, I knew I could take it to my husband. Even if he didn't understand why it was a big deal to me, he offered me comfort anyway. And if something went wrong for him, he would give me a blow-by-blow, and I could encourage him.

But what about now, Father? I know you're always with me, and you are even more interested in the details of my life than my husband was. That still hasn't stopped me from missing *his* input. And though I'm happy he is where he is, I feel a twinge of sadness that he no longer needs me as a listening ear.

As I hunger for him, I think of how you referred to yourself as "the bread of life." Surely that's more than sandwich bread and has to do with other types of hunger . . . maybe even soul-hunger. Could it be my husband-hunger is really that? Because if it is, longing for him will never fill me. It would be like trying to satisfy a sweet tooth with potato chips.

14

> [The LORD] satisfies the thirsty
>
> and fills the hungry with good things.
>
> Psalm 107:9

Father, please fill me up—even if I don't exactly know with what. Those conversations with my husband filled me with a special satisfaction. He was willing to listen and respond, because he loved me.

Now that I think about it, though, *you* are willing to listen and respond out of love too. Your Word says your ears are always open to my cries. Your advice is always flawless, and you have an answer to every problem. I don't know why I never thought of you that way before.

Maybe, even as I miss the camaraderie of my husband, I can be satisfied by connecting with you in much the same way. Though I miss hearing *his* voice, maybe I can learn to hear *yours*. Your words will come through the pages of the Bible and also directly into my heart, conscience, and will, by your Spirit.

I may need time to practice conversing with you. I'm beginning to understand that my husband-hunger, which is so natural for a widow, can no longer to satisfied. But my soul-hunger, a supernatural thing, can be fully satisfied through you.

Let's talk more and more, Father. As I feed on conversation with you, I'm pretty sure my hunger pains will subside.

In the name of Jesus I pray. Amen.

Jesus declared, "I am the bread of life.

Whoever comes to me will never go hungry."

John 6:35

FLY FISHING

My soul is weary with sorrow;

strengthen me according to your word.

Psalm 119:28

DEAR FATHER,

WHEN I FIRST BECAME a widow, I doubted I would survive. The longing to be with my husband was so strong, I hoped I would die, too. There was something appealing about that idea, since it would bring us together again.

But common sense finally surfaced, telling me how selfish that was. It would mean throwing the rest of our family into a second wave of grief that would threaten to overwhelm them. And once I thought of it that way, I knew I'd have to press forward as a widow. So here I am, Father, floundering. I want to show my family that your grace is sufficient, but I'm not always doing that very well.

Moving through sorrow is hard work. I come to the end of some days so exhausted I can hardly get ready for bed. I don't feel like I've accomplished anything all day long . . . nothing except a day's worth of grieving, which is unpleasant, tiring work.

I feel careworn and depleted much of the time, Lord, and need your sustenance more and more. Originally, I thought the situation would get better and better as time passed, with the burdens becoming less and less. Why hasn't that happened?

> Cast your cares on the Lord and he will sustain you;
>
> he will never let the righteous be shaken.
>
> Psalm 55:22

My load of grief seems to be getting heavier. But maybe that's because, without realizing it, I'm not letting you help me carry it. There's a Bible verse that invites me to "cast" my cares on you. It's an attention-grabbing word picture, Father. I see someone fly-fishing, throwing a line as far away as possible—which might be exactly what you want me to do with my widow-burdens.

I'm trying to deal with the reality I've been given—in one sense, it was given by you. I'm not blaming you, Father, just acknowledging your sovereignty. You could have let my husband live longer than he did, but you didn't. Coming to this realization has done something positive for me. It helps me understand one reason you're offering to take over the problems that come with widowhood. Because you allowed it, you'll escort me through it.

Please help me to cast and re-cast my worries toward you, right when they come to mind, acknowledging your power over my situation. As I practice, I'm fairly sure my casting skills will improve. And I have confidence that eventually you'll bring me to a brand-new version of widowhood, one with far less tension and much more joy.

In the name of Jesus I pray. Amen.

May the God of hope fill you with all joy and peace as you trust in him, so that you may overflow with hope by the power of the Holy Spirit.

Romans 15:13

RACING TOWARD CONTENTMENT

Let us run with perseverance the race marked out for us, fixing our eyes on Jesus, the pioneer and perfecter of faith.

Hebrews 12:1–2

DEAR FATHER,

SOMETIMES I WISH I could walk around with blinders on, like a country horse in city traffic, eyes protected from all the disturbing distractions. It might be a good idea if the worries of widowhood were blocked from my view. I would stress less and could concentrate more on moving straight ahead. Knowing me, though, I'd probably crane my neck to look side-to-side anyway.

My mood slips into the what-if's of widowhood the minute I look at the worrisome dilemmas around me. And I do that all too easily. Why does worry come so naturally while contentment is usually elusive?

In your Word, Father, you entrusted your biggest assignments to people who were good at focusing on their end goals—the goals you set for them. They were content to fight battles, rule nations, prophesy bad news, and endure persecution, all while remaining intent on the assignments you gave them. If they could do that, surely I can do widowhood.

> I have learned the secret of being content in any and every situation. . . . I can do all this through him who gives me strength.
>
> Philippians 4:12–13

If I want to follow you faithfully, I need to make up my mind to let nothing interfere with that. I really want to do what you want me to do—no matter how hard it is.

A great example of this was Jesus, even though his goal was the agony of the cross. He didn't need blinders to keep Him focused but was all-in from the very beginning. Even at the tender age of twelve, when He told His parents He was about His "Father's business," Jesus was already stalwart in His march toward the ministry you'd given Him.

What would it take for me to be like that, Father? The tasks you've assigned me aren't nearly as tough as His, and you've even offered to help me accomplish them. But I know success means doing away with the what-if's and if-only's. You'll want me to stop wishing I could go back to the days when I still had my husband. And I'll need to purposefully count blessings rather than losses, tackling each widow-dilemma with perseverance.

Help me to think of widowhood not as a sad end but as the start of something new, something different *you're* doing, in and around me. Please show me how to be content right in the middle of it, without succumbing to the disturbing distractions.

In the name of Jesus I pray. Amen.

One thing I do, forgetting those things which are behind

and reaching forward to those things which are ahead . . .

Philippians 3:13 (NKJV)

FEELING SMALL

When I consider your heavens . . .

what is mankind that you are mindful of them,

human beings that you care for them?

Psalm 8:3–4

DEAR FATHER,

SOMETIMES WHEN I'M OUT walking late at night, I feel lonely and small. And I wonder if my sad circumstances have slipped past your notice. I look up at the stars and the enormity of the heavens and think, "How could you care about little old me, with everything else going on in your universe?"

Not that your omniscience is limited in any way, but I struggle to believe I'm all that important to you. You're the One who keeps the earth spinning and holds the stars in place, amazing feats of supernatural power. But how can my concerns, by comparison, be anything but trivial to you?

[The Lord says,] "See, I have engraved you on the palms of my hands."

Isaiah 49:16

But when I read the Bible, I see you're not only aware of my situation, you've also "written me down" as a sign you won't forget about me. This amazing fact, that you want to tenderly care for me as I struggle to shift from married to widowed, is a huge comfort. It's a promise I know I should store at the forefront of my mind.

Father, you made humans unique, the only created beings with souls. More importantly, we're the only ones your Son died to save. That's reason enough to classify us in a different category of care than everything else you made and manage. The twinkling stars, as beautiful and plentiful as they are, don't have souls. Could that be the reason you capably run the entire universe yet still have a desire to care for me?

Truly you are a God of wonders. I want to believe you see me in my grief—right into my soul and heart—and that you tend to my concerns in the same extraordinary way you tend to the details of the heavens. Because mankind is the best of your creation, I don't doubt you're taking extra care to oversee what happens to each of us. How remarkable that you, Almighty God, are willing to minister to my personal needs. I am in awe!

In my darkest hours, please remind me of the profound one-on-one relationship we have. And would you please keep me from ever doubting it? I hope that while I'm out walking late at night and find myself gazing at the heavens, I'll no longer feel small or insignificant by comparison. May your stars serve as sparkling reminders of your faithful, loving care for me.

In the name of Jesus I pray. Amen.

[Jesus said,] "What is the price of five sparrows—two copper coins? Yet God does not forget a single one of them. . . . So don't be afraid; you are more valuable to God than a whole flock of sparrows."

Luke 12:6–7 (NLT)

TRAUMA ON A TIMELINE

"I am the Alpha and the Omega," says the Lord God,

"who is, and who was, and who is to come."

Revelation 1:8

DEAR FATHER,

WHEN I THINK ABOUT my life, I see it much like a line on a graph, with peaks and valleys somewhat like those on a heart monitor. Some shoot upward, sudden and sharp. These points in my past have usually included pain. Others are gradual, slow-rising and gentle, situations I saw coming and could prepare for. These hurt less.

Currently my line is on such an abrupt rise it threatens to go off the monitor. Though I suspected widowhood was coming, I had no idea how to brace myself for its misery and couldn't guess how rough it was going to get. As it's turning out, this peak compares to no other.

Father, I appreciate knowing you stood at the beginning of my graph line back when my life began—and you are already standing at the end of it. I believe you, Father, when you say you always have been and you ever will be. To know that my unknowns are known to you gives me a strong sense of security, and I'm thankful, Lord.

I'm also grateful you've given me more than just your "Alpha and Omega" statement. You've promised to be close to me between my beginning and ending, and you say it in ways I can understand.

> You hem me in behind and before,
>
> and you lay your hand upon me.
>
> 944Psalm 139:5
>
> . . . and underneath are the everlasting arms.
>
> Deuteronomy 33:27

You've said your presence literally surrounds me, Father, so on days when I'm feeling nervous or scared, it helps me to picture that. I try to sense you following behind me, watching my back; walking in front of me, leading the way; touching me from above, protecting me from harm; cradling me from beneath, preventing me from falling.

Knowing you completely encircle me is a boost of courage like no other. My mental graph line with its jagged spike of widowhood still burdens me. But then I think of how some people love to climb—the more challenging the peak, the better their experience. With you surrounding me as you are, maybe I can begin to view this graph-line climb as a strange, new type of adventure.

Some people appreciate mountains simply for their beauty. Is it possible, Father, you'll allow me to experience a bit of beauty as I continue hiking into widowhood?

Surely, one day I'll make my way back down the other side of this steep peak and will have conquered the challenge because of you. Whatever I see along the way, I pray that you and I will grow closer than ever as we journey on together.

In the name of Jesus I pray. Amen.

> As the mountains surround Jerusalem,
>
> so the LORD surrounds his people
>
> both now and forevermore.
>
> Psalm 125:2

PART 2

FIGHTING
My Fears

FRUSTRATED BY FEAR

Have no fear of sudden disaster

or of the ruin that overtakes the wicked,

for the LORD will be at your side

and will keep your foot from being snared.

Proverbs 3:25–26

DEAR FATHER,

I REALIZE NO ONE is completely fearless. One person might fear bugs while another brushes them away. Someone else might fear crowds while another loves to meet new people. But now, as I struggle with widowhood, fears I've never known are surfacing from someplace deep inside.

In my more rational moments, I know these fears are silly, since most of them aren't grounded in reality. You know, Father, how ridiculous it is for a grown woman to be afraid of the dark or suspect of strangers. But that's who I've become.

I've heard it's not unusual, after a husband dies, for fear to rise in a widow's heart—especially during the night. Lord, I know such fear isn't logical, since most men aren't warriors and haven't fought an enemy to protect their wives. Yet when our husbands are with us, we women feel safer.

It doesn't make sense, but I find myself succumbing to that kind of fear, even when my mind tells me I shouldn't. If my husband returned, I'd probably feel protected, just as I did before he left. Why is that?

This is what the LORD says . . .

"Do not fear, for I have redeemed you;

I have summoned you by name; you are mine."

Isaiah 43:1

I know I belong to you, Lord. You've received my husband into heaven and, since you've redeemed us both, you'll someday receive me too. But that is then. This is now. How do I cope with *these* days and *these* nights?

In your Word you don't casually suggest we eliminate fear; you command it. Again and again, you say, "Do not fear," urging us to have confidence in you. But how do I keep these unreasonable emotions from dominating me? How do I cooperate with your command?

One thing I know for sure: all my anxious striving hasn't gotten me anywhere. I need a new approach, Father. Maybe I should talk with other widows, people who've faced their fears with courage. Mostly, though, I should probably just keep talking to you, trusting you to walk through my fears with me. As I do, I pray you'll give me the confidence I need to make it easier next time, and the time after that.

I'm certain that you love me, Father. That's why it's frustrating to be so fearful. I'd rather stand tall, knowing you and I will walk shoulder-to-shoulder into, and out of, every fear-inducing situation. My trust has to be in you. Maybe the more I learn to trust, the less I'll be afraid. Please make it so.

In the name of Jesus I pray. Amen.

When I am afraid, I put my trust in you.

In God, whose word I praise—in God I trust and am not afraid.

Psalm 56:3–4

EXPENSIVE GRIEF

Why, my soul, are you downcast?

Why so disturbed within me?

Put your hope in God, for I will yet praise him,

my Savior and my God.

Psalm 43:5

DEAR FATHER,

I'M BEGINNING TO REALIZE that grief is expensive. It forces the spending of emotional energy that is already in short supply. When that happens, it takes everything in me to cling to hope. And sometimes I wonder what I'm even hoping for. It isn't always clear.

I guess I'm hoping for less sadness and more joy. That's probably what everyone hopes for, not just those of us who've lost someone special. But surely even a lonely widow ought to be able to hope for something specific. Would you define that for me, Father?

I know I'm supposed to hope in you, Lord, but I'm not sure what that means. Would personal happiness be part of it? I hope I can one day be happy again, as I was when my husband was with me. And though I know my hope can't be in him, I have trouble anticipating happiness in any other way than being his wife.

Love the Lord, all his faithful people!

The Lord preserves those who are true to him. . . .

Be strong and take heart,

all you who hope in the Lord.

Psalm 31:23–24

But he's gone. For good. And I need to stop backwards-hoping like that. Instead I should do what your Word suggests: hope in you, both for the present and the future. Even into eternity. So what does that look like today?

If I trust you to watch over my dwindling emotional bank account, will you make regular deposits into it? Will you let me share in your emotional riches, since you have an abundance of everything? Or will you simply deliver whatever I need on any given day? I know you'll provide, as long as my hope for rescue is in you, not in myself or anyone else. Surely you know all about my emotional overdrafts and how depleted I can get.

As I learn to hope for your provision, Father, I know I'll have to pour out my heart in complete candor. I'll need to invite you to move into the dark corners of my soul where no one else has been invited to go. Even I haven't gone to some of those places yet, Lord. But please give me the will to be fully honest with you, in a way I never have before.

I know I can trust you to get me through this difficult time. And when the crisis of adjustment has passed, you might even deposit a surplus into my emotional bank account. If you do, perhaps I'll one day be able to draw on it to benefit others who are hurting, too. Thank you in advance, Father. Such a possibility gives me great hope.

In the name of Jesus I pray. Amen.

> Trust in him at all times, you people;
>
> pour out your hearts to him, for God is our refuge.
>
> Psalm 62:8

FEELING WOBBLY

"Everyone who hears these words of mine

and puts them into practice

is like a wise man who built his house on the rock."

Matthew 7:24

DEAR FATHER,

SOMETIMES I HAVE THE funny feeling the ground is trembling beneath me. From what I understand, earthquakes feel just like that. People stop what they're doing and stand stock-still, trying to define the movement. Is it beneath me? Or inside me?

In my case, the wobbling isn't an earthquake or even a balance problem. It's the shifting of my life's foundation as I move from married to widowed.

It reminds me of an old Sunday school story about two builders, one wise and the other foolish. The wise man built on a rock, and the foolish man chose sand. When the storm came, we all knew which house was going down.

That's why the movement in my foundation is so unsettling, Lord. When you led me to my husband so many years ago, I thought that since we built our marriage on Christian principles, we were grounded on a rock. Now that he's gone, though, I'm feeling wobbly. Is it possible we built on our own ideas and not directly on you? Did we inadvertently build on shifting sand?

It feels like the rains have come down, the floods have come up—and my house has fallen. What am I missing, Lord? Were we so enamored with each other that we somehow left you out of our foundation? Could that be the reason I feel so shaky without my husband? And if that's true, what do I do now?

> From the ends of the earth I call to you,
>
> I call as my heart grows faint;
>
> lead me to the rock that is higher than I.
>
> Psalm 61:2

Feeling wobbly is no fun. It's upsetting and makes me think that *I* might fall like that biblical house. I need your stability more than ever, Father, and want to be a widow whose feet are firmly planted on you as my foundation, my rock.

The example of the two builders tells me I should hear your words and put them into practice. Please help me to listen for what you're saying to me through this story. Then, once I have your instructions, help me to follow them as carefully as a builder follows a blueprint.

I guess it isn't all that complicated. It's listen first and obey after that. If I do those two things, my life will be constructed on you, my foundational Rock—and I'll wobble no more. Thank you, Father. Please enable me to do it exactly that way.

In the name of Jesus I pray. Amen.

He will be the sure foundation for your times,

a rich store of salvation and wisdom and knowledge;

the fear of the LORD is the key to this treasure.

Isaiah 33:6

SEEKING AND CALLING

Do not hide your face from me when I am in distress.

Turn your ear to me; when I call, answer me quickly.

Psalm 102:2

DEAR FATHER,

SOMETIMES I FEEL LIKE you're ignoring me, as if you've made a decision to put my life on autopilot for a while. I know that's not really true, but when troubles pile up, that's what it feels like.

You've said if I seek you, you'll let yourself be found, and if I call to you, you'll answer me. I'm seeking and calling, but nothing seems to be happening. What am I doing wrong?

I know you want me to cultivate patience, especially when I'm waiting for you to answer my prayers. But if you would just give me a tiny glimpse of you, I know it would improve my ability to wait.

> The cords of death entangled me,
>
> the anguish of the grave came over me;
>
> I was overcome by distress and sorrow.
>
> Then I called on the name of the LORD.
>
> Psalm 116:3–4

Why is it so difficult to trust you when I don't hear your voice or see your plan? I don't think I'm second-guessing my commitment to you, and I sure don't question your supremacy. So is it the timing that bothers me? When you seem distant, I can't understand why the separation between us has to last so long. Why do I have to wait at all to see or hear you?

Because you're outside of time, Father, the passing of days and weeks is never an issue for you. Your timelessness lets you view my life—from conception to death—as a single image. You have a big-picture perspective which allows you to lead me and show yourself according to my specific needs. I'm sure all your purposes for me will be met. But when I can't see or hear you, my finite mind says, "Is He going to act? What if He leaves me hanging?"

Sometimes I'm tempted to jump to that wrong conclusion, and "tempted" is the correct word. Surely that's the enemy's intention, to make me doubt you're going to respond to me. Then when I get frustrated and impatient, he gets happy.

Seeing things in that light does make it a bit easier to wait on you. I don't want the devil to have even a smidgen of victory in my life, especially now that I'm a widow. He probably knows I need you more than ever and would love to weaken my faith in you. So please strengthen my resolve to be patient, Father. Remind me every day that when I can't see or hear you, you are still hard at work on my behalf.

In the name of Jesus I pray. Amen.

I trust in you, [Lord, my God];

do not let me be put to shame, nor let my enemies triumph

over me. No one who hopes in you will ever be put to shame.

Psalm 25:2–3

HAUNTING REGRETS

Let each person lead the life that the Lord has assigned to him, and to which God has called him.

1 Corinthians 7:17 (ESV)

DEAR FATHER,

LATELY I'VE BEEN STRUGGLING with regrets, the would-have's, could-have's, and should-have's of my relationship with my husband. No amount of hindsight can rearrange what's already been said between us . . . or left unsaid. And because my man is completely unreachable now, I can't even apologize or ask for a chance to do better.

As I remember details of our time together, my mind often focuses on my thoughtlessness. It's as if there's a yellow highlighter in my head underscoring only the negatives. I know I did many things right, but these days all I can think of is my mistakes.

Every day I harshly judge the wife I was and worry I might have taken my husband for granted. A good wife always looks for chances to praise her partner. Did I do that? I know that expressing gratitude builds a strong marriage relationship, but I'm not sure I did enough of it. And even when I genuinely appreciated him, I often failed to voice it.

These questions are haunting me, Lord, and my list of perceived failures seems to grow daily. I don't know how to get out from under these feelings, since I'm powerless now to make corrections. Can you help me?

> Therefore, there is now no condemnation
>
> for those who are in Christ Jesus.
>
> Romans 8:1

I'm glad you don't judge me for my thoughtlessness, but is there any way I can actually right my wrongs? Your Word says our tongues can either soothe or harm, but neglecting to say what I should have said probably falls closer to harm. Maybe a way to negate my failures is to succeed at thanking, complimenting, and encouraging the people who are still in my life today.

I realize that speaking the right words has your power to uplift others, and I want to get better at it. But I won't be able to speak those good words unless you pluck them from my brain and set them on my tongue.

Maybe if you prompt me again and again, the process will become easier and feel more natural. I pray it might even ease my guilt over the good thoughts I so often failed to put into words for my husband.

Is that what you have in mind, Lord—positive words for others and a little blessing for me, too? If so, let me practice right now by saying thanks to *you* for giving me a way to improve on my past. You always know exactly what I need.

In the name of Jesus I pray. Amen.

"I the LORD search the heart and examine the mind,

to reward each person according to their conduct,

according to what their deeds deserve."

Jeremiah 17:10

AFRAID OF FEAR

If you say, "The LORD is my refuge,"

and you make the Most High your dwelling . . .

he will command his angels concerning you

to guard you in all your ways.

Psalm 91:9, 11

DEAR FATHER,

WHENEVER I HAVE A miserable night that seems to last forever, I'm always glad to see the eastern sky lighten. It's not that I don't go to bed tired. You know how exhausting grief can be. But sometimes I hear strange sounds in the wee small hours.

I'm very familiar with the sounds my house makes: the furnace starting up, the fridge humming, the wind on my windows. But now, when I think I hear something unusual, I'm tempted to call 911. In my mind's eye I picture a black-clad intruder rummaging through my drawers and cabinets. I fully expect to see my bedroom doorknob turn.

Fear never tormented me when my husband was in the house, but now I feel like a sitting duck. Does that mean I don't trust you to care for me, Father? Maybe so.

Your Word promises safety. You talk about angels guarding us and claim that no threatening circumstance will overwhelm us. But what I see on the news seems to say otherwise. How can I resolve those contradictions?

> When you are on your beds, search your hearts and be silent.
>
> Offer the sacrifices of the righteous and trust in the LORD.
>
> Psalm 4:4–5

I want to trust you, Father, especially during the night, but I need to know what you mean when you say you'll protect me. I know I'm not immune to difficulties; I just wish I was strong enough to rely on you in the midst of them.

Obviously, since so many people suffer harm, your promises of protection don't guarantee physical safety. Might you be referring to soul-safety? If that's it, I still don't know what to do with the fear that keeps me trembling during the night.

Is it possible I'm supposed to trust you even as my adrenalin is surging? If I made the first move toward trust, would you then infuse me with your supernatural composure—even while I'm still scared? I can't imagine having such a radical faith, Lord. It can only happen if you take my shaky trust and steady it by your power.

Maybe some faith-exercise would help. If so, the next question is, Am I willing? Oh Lord, I do want to trust you, but in fearful circumstances it doesn't come naturally.

So let me try something new. The next time I'm afraid, I'll attempt to exercise my trust-muscle with the expectation that you'll immediately slow my heartbeat and fill me with calm. It'll go against everything in me at that moment, but I do want to try. Please, Lord, come through for me.

In the name of Jesus I pray. Amen.

"Whoever listens to me will dwell secure and will be at ease, without dread of disaster."

Proverbs 1:33 (ESV)

PART 3

ASKING
New Questions

SELFISH SORROW

Commit everything you do to the LORD.

Trust him, and he will help you.

Psalm 37:5 (NLT)

DEAR FATHER,

I LOVE YOU. And I believe you are the one true God of the universe. Your promises are true, and when you say something is going to happen, it does. That means when you say you're going to help me, you will.

Sometimes I feel bad that in my widowhood I'm not a better example of how a daughter of yours should respond to your words. I wish I could feel more comfort than I do through the promises of Scripture. It's not that I don't believe they're true. It's that I see myself as an exception to them. I feel like I can't experience peace and joy during this trial because, after all, I've lost my husband. And that's a big deal.

So I'm wondering, Lord, is my skewed thinking a result of selfishness? Am I in the middle of a pity party? If that's the case, I need you to show me how to change my perspective. Because until I do, I won't be able to take advantage of all the help you offer.

> Consider it pure joy, my brothers and sisters,
>
> whenever you face trials of many kinds,
>
> because you know that the testing of your faith produces
>
> perseverance.
>
> James 1:2–3

I know that struggles and troubles aren't always a bad thing, since genuine good can come from them. And I don't want to forfeit that good by acting selfishly while I'm trying to adjust to widowhood. But it's difficult to get out from under this self-focus I feel. I do sense you're monitoring my situation closely, Lord, and are aware of my feelings. I'm so glad! And I'm thankful I never have to hide my emotions from you, but can be honest and open.

I don't want to feel sorry for myself, Father. I know that focusing on my difficulties is much like disregarding your close presence and your endless kindness to me. Deep down, I want to take advantage of everything you offer and be victorious right in the middle of my new life as a widow. I believe you want that, too. But that means I'll need to give up my way of handling grief and surrender to yours.

Father, I want to leave all the decisions up to you, and I'm pleading with you to give me the right outlook. Please tell me which Scriptures to read. Renew my mind through your Spirit's power. Change my self-centered response to circumstances into gratitude for you and your blessings. Please remind me every day that my life shouldn't revolve around the absence of my husband but around the presence of my Lord.

In the name of Jesus I pray. Amen.

I consider everything a loss because of the surpassing worth of knowing Christ Jesus my Lord.

Philippians 3:8

A FOREST OF QUESTION MARKS

When times are good, be happy;

but when times are bad, consider this:

God has made the one as well as the other.

Therefore, no one can discover

anything about their future.

Ecclesiastes 7:14

DEAR FATHER,

I'M NOT SURE WHAT tomorrow will bring. Or today, for that matter. When I think about my future weeks and months as a widow, I'm not sure about any of them. And it's upsetting not to know how things are going to go.

I once thought I knew what my future would look like: growing old with my husband who I loved dearly; shouldering the burdens of old age and maybe poor health, but doing it together; talking over decisions and coming to agreeable conclusions; adding to our long marriage history . . . as a twosome.

But here I am, without my husband beside me, walking into a forest of question marks. Father, can you encourage me with an answer or two about my future?

I know you are the God of opportunity, and my becoming a widow didn't change that. So, Lord, I'm asking for a new beginning. I'm trusting you to open doors I never even thought about walking through. I have a hunch you're going to bring new experiences that will astound me. And, little by little, I'm hoping the question marks will be replaced with answers.

Though my current circumstances hint otherwise, I really believe my tomorrows have the potential to become bright again. That's true for only one reason: you will be there beside me.

Years ago people sang, "I know who holds the future, and I know he holds my hand." Of course that's you, Father. I know you've got a good grip on both my future and my hand. Please make that real to me, especially on the days when my tears are flowing.

I want very much to please you, Lord, and to be an example to others of how to grieve with hope as you say believers should. But I'll need an extra dose of your optimism at the beginning of each new day in order to blend the loss of my husband with a hope for my future without him.

Most of all, I'll need to know you're leading me through that forest of question marks in front of me. And though I'll have to wait patiently for your answers, right now please assure me you're carefully monitoring each unknown. Once I'm sure of that, I know everything will work out fine.

In the name of Jesus I pray. Amen.

Let the morning bring me word of your unfailing love,

for I have put my trust in you.

Show me the way I should go,

for to you I entrust my life.

Psalm 143:8

MENTAL POPCORN

We know and rely on the love God has for us.

There is no fear in love. . . .

Perfect love drives out fear.

1 John 4:16, 18

DEAR FATHER,

ONCE IN A WHILE, I become fearful about something, so I'm coming to you for help. My concern is that I'll have so much trouble adjusting to widowhood, it will become my permanent identity. Sometimes it seems sensible to leave my husband's things exactly as he left them . . . indefinitely. But that sounds to me like getting stuck—which is exactly what I'm afraid of.

Also, what if I can't make the mental shift from married to single? And what if I'm unable to do the things my husband used to do for us as a couple? And what if I'm never able to empty his drawers or give away his clothes?

I apologize for all the questions, Father. But sometimes my mind feels like a bag of popcorn, with kernels flying every which way. These troubling thoughts and questions refuse to quiet down. Apparently I've become one of those widow-oxymorons with my mind in constant motion and the rest of me completely stuck.

Oh Father, I know this probably sounds like nonsense. What's happening to me? What will it take for me to accept this new reality without it overwhelming me? How can I silence all the questions? And will I ever be able to see myself as more than just a sad widow?

> "Do not be afraid; you will . . .
>
> remember no more the reproach of your widowhood."
>
> Isaiah 54:4

I know you're able to sort out the confusion in my head, Father. You can bring tranquility where there's bewilderment and see to it that I won't be forever fixed in the intense mourning of early widowhood. What I don't understand is how I can be set free from sadness and still be able to think about my husband.

When I try to figure it all out, I only get more mental popcorn. So I'm bringing this problem to you, desperate for your rescue. I have faith that you can and eventually will bring me to a place of composure. I don't know how or when, but I know you will.

Please be my stability, Father. And would you send along other stable influences too? I'm not very good at asking for support, knowing people are already overloaded without adding my concerns to theirs. But you can do this with expertise.

You can prompt a friend to send a text or note at just the right time. And you can slow down my jumpy thoughts by reminding me of Scripture's promises. Please soothe my worn-out mind, Lord, and somehow prevent me from getting stuck in my grief. I'm counting on you.

In the name of Jesus I pray. Amen.

The one who calls you is faithful, and he will do it.

1 Thessalonians 5:24

WHAT TO DO?

The heart of the discerning acquires knowledge,

for the ears of the wise seek it out.

Proverbs 18:15

DEAR FATHER,

I'M WORKING HARD TO make the seismic mental shift from being married to being a widow. It's a difficult process. My first inclination is to do what I've always done: ask my husband for help. I long for his counsel as I break this new ground. Of course, if he were here to advise me, I wouldn't be struggling with widowhood.

My head spins with this round-and-round logic much of the time, and I hope it's not a permanent part of my new life. On everyday matters, sound judgment seems to have flown out the window—and when a decision, however big or small, needs to be made, I often can't do it. This is frightening, and I sometimes wonder if I'm losing my mind.

Please don't let me lose my mind, Lord. I long for *you* to control my thoughts, especially to curb them when they head in a fearful direction. You've urged me to be brave and not to fear the many changes I must make.

> "Be strong and courageous.
>
> Do not be afraid or terrified . . .
>
> for the LORD your God goes with you;
>
> he will never leave you nor forsake you."
>
> Deuteronomy 31:6

I know that as circumstances around me change, I'm going to have to change, too. When my husband died, the biggest shift was moving from married to single—admitting that my marriage had ended. I can't believe you would let that happen without a Plan B. Some say all of your plans are Plan A, but believing widowhood is your first choice for me is difficult to accept.

Am I arguing with you, Lord? Or whining? Please forgive me if it seems that way. I just need to know what my next steps ought to be. Plant your desires in my mind, so I'll know how to cope with the stresses of this new life. Transform me into the widow you want me to be.

Since I don't have my husband here to counsel me or help me adjust, what would you suggest? If I have to make a decision or think things through in a new way, of course I'll ask you first—but might your help also come through another person? With enough coaching from you and others, maybe I'll eventually learn to handle this new life as an independent woman.

Thank you for encouraging me with these thoughts, Father. I feel a little better already.

In the name of Jesus I pray. Amen.

Be transformed by the renewing of your mind.

Then you will be able to test and approve what God's will is—

his good, pleasing and perfect will.

Romans 12:2

HASHING IT OVER

"If anyone is a worshiper of God and does his will, God listens to him."

John 9:31 (ESV)

DEAR FATHER,

AS I TALK WITH you in prayer, I usually make a request and then watch for your answer, which often seems long in coming. But you're probably thinking, "My delay has big benefits—one of which is that you'll continue to spend time with me about that request."

Actually, meeting with you, Father, is the loftier purpose of all my prayers, more important than even the asking or receiving. Talking brings us together in a unique way. Where else can we share one-on-one time like we do in the quiet privacy of prayer?

When I think about it that way, I can almost picture you waiting for me to extract myself from the whirlwind of life—separating from everything and everyone else with the sole purpose of drawing close to you. And when I finally reach you, I can let out a deep sigh as I sit down at your feet to talk and listen. That's probably the closest I'll get to you, this side of heaven.

Sometimes when you delay answering my prayers, I feel frustration and disappointment. I confess that such feelings are inappropriate. Please help me instead to be intentionally glad—glad that we can continue talking about my concerns, improving on my requests or possibly eliminating them altogether. Please direct me, Father, as I try to see things from your point of view. When you require me to wait, I'm sure you're hoping my requests will become less selfish and line up better with your will.

Besides, by spending time with you, I'm identifying with you in a unique way that benefits me greatly—with or without answers to prayer. Your Word says you find delight in my coming to you, so I want to show up faithfully, and often.

> Trust in the LORD and do good;
>
> dwell in the land and enjoy safe pasture. . . .
>
> Be still before the LORD and wait patiently for him.
>
> Psalm 37:3, 7

Thank you for the love you have for me, Father. I don't deserve it. I'll always try to approach you with a heart of gratitude and an attitude of patience. And if I should ever come with a demanding edge in my voice, please correct me firmly. That you allow me into your presence at all is a gift beyond my understanding.

I don't know why you invite me into your inner circle, Father. Sometimes it's just you, your Son, your Spirit . . . and me. Unfathomable! My heart is bursting over such a privilege. May I never forget that better than any answer to prayer is simply spending time with you.

In the name of Jesus I pray, Amen.

Come near to God and he will come near to you. . . .

Humble yourselves before the Lord, and he will lift you up.

James 4:8, 10

FULLY ALIVE

God, being rich in mercy

because of the great love with which he loved us . . .

made us alive together with Christ.

Ephesians 2:4–5 (ESV)

DEAR FATHER,

WIDOWHOOD POSES A VARIETY of problems—not the least of which is my constant inner focus. All I think about is losing my husband and how sad that's made me feel. This continual introspection just can't be good. Is it *ever* productive to lead a life consumed with self?

Your Word tells me to square off with whatever comes each day, to persevere through difficulties. Widowhood is, at best, a difficulty, one that makes it hard to persevere. I'm tempted to feel sorry for myself, and think that somehow I'll feel better as a result. But it doesn't seem to work that way.

When I focus daily on my sadness, I place my own dilemma as my top priority, and the result is a growing sense of entitlement. Sometimes I expect everyone else to care about my loss as much as I do, which of course they can't. Such thinking isn't even rational, and if it was, it wouldn't help heal my heart anyway. It might even slow my progress.

There's a verse in your Word that tells me to pick up my cross daily and follow you. Could it be that widowhood is the cross you want me to carry right now? So if I determined to take on widowhood without expecting special attention from you or anyone else, would this somehow honor you and make life better for me?

> "If any of you wants to be my follower,
>
> you must turn from your selfish ways,
>
> take up your cross, and follow me."
>
> Matthew 16:24 (NLT)

Much of what you teach us about successful living is contrary to human logic, Father. My struggle to adjust to life without my husband seems to be one of those things. It's no fun to deny myself the inner focus I want to have, in favor of taking up widowhood without complaint. But apparently that's what I need to do if I'm going to manage the way you want me to. And I really do want that, Lord.

Maybe I should view these days as an opportunity to stand out from the crowd. Please show me how to grieve my loss while simultaneously following you instead of withdrawing from or blaming you. Maybe it's my chance to be a good example of walking by faith and not by sight. My intense self-focus has probably been working against that.

Please show me, Father, how and where I'm living my life contrary to your plans for me. I especially need you to bring order inside my head. Then, as I learn how you want me to think about widowhood, I can focus less on me and more on you. And that, I'm sure, will bring progress.

In the name of Jesus I pray. Amen.

It is God who works in you to will and to act

in order to fulfill his good purpose.

Philippians 2:13

PART 4

RECOGNIZING
God's Touch

HAND IN HAND

I cling to you; your right hand upholds me.

Psalm 63:8

DEAR FATHER,

I'M VERY THANKFUL THERE are many ways you teach me what you want me to know. You've put hundreds of word pictures into the Bible, and each one helps me understand you a little better. One image you use again and again is of your "strong arm" or "right hand" working for my benefit. You also write about your hand holding tightly to mine.

Holding onto someone can be either negative or positive. If I've got a grip on a small child who's trying to run off, she'll squirm and tug in an effort to get free. But if two lovers are arm in arm or hand in hand, neither wants to break such an enjoyable attachment.

That's the kind of holding I hope you and I can do, Father. Although I'm dependent on you much like a child depends on her parents, I hope always to be eager for your hold on me. As long as you and I are joined together, arm in arm or hand in hand, I know my emotional strength will never run out and my inner courage won't wane. Fear won't have its way with me, and I'll never forget you are close by.

> "I am the LORD your God
>
> who takes hold of your right hand and says to you,
>
> Do not fear; I will help you."
>
> Isaiah 41:13

There's a beautiful word picture in the poem "Footprints." It describes two sets of prints in the sand until suddenly one disappears. That, the poet wrote, was when you carried the person who was too weak to walk. I know that's an image of what you want to do for me. When I'm about to fall, you'll carry me until I'm strong enough to walk again.

The Bible has one other visual that's not always easy to look at. It depicts you looking me in the eye and telling me what you want me to do. And I don't always want to comply: case-in-point, widowhood. But in this picture you're hoping I will say, "My life is in your hands, Lord."

Please put that picture into my mind each day, Lord, no matter how hard the reality is. May I never squirm in your grip or try to tug my arm away from yours. Instead, Father, may I step close enough to wrap *my* arms around you.

In the name of Jesus I pray. Amen.

Though I am surrounded by troubles . . .

you reach out your hand, and the power of your right hand

saves me.

Psalm 138:7 (NLT)

TELLING THE TRUTH

"I am the Alpha and the Omega,

the Beginning and the End."

Revelation 21:6

DEAR FATHER,

TODAY, AS ON MANY days, my heart is heavy. The reason this time is that I feel I owe you an apology. One of my first thoughts this morning was what a mixed-up mess my life is without my husband, since everything has changed. But almost immediately I felt bad about summarizing things in such a derogatory way.

Maybe that was you catching my attention, Father, prompting me to examine the situation more closely. I could almost hear you saying, "You think *everything* has changed? Is that true?"

And of course it isn't. I'm sorry for indulging in such a sweeping exaggeration. It's probably an indication that I'm not depending on you like I should. My marriage has ended, yes. Like a stone tossed into a lake, that one change has had a ripple effect, setting off many others. But the whole truth is that much in my life has stayed the same.

I still have family who love me and each other. I still have the same tenderhearted friends. I still have a nice place to live. And best of all I still have you, my most faithful Friend.

And there's more. You, Lord, haven't changed and never will. You haven't stopped keeping your promises, and you're still watching over me. Your Spirit hasn't stopped comforting me, and your love for me is still strong. You are still running your universe, and still performing wonders every day.

> "I the LORD do not change."
>
> Malachi 3:6

Thank you, Father, for being rock solid. You're showing me that the list of what hasn't changed is far longer than the list of what has. I'm sorry I've been so wrapped up in my troubles I haven't been properly aware of you. I badly need you to broaden my narrow horizon. Most days, though, I can't envision that happening unless you first heal my grief. Have I got that wrong?

Maybe I should try to focus on you and your phenomenal abilities rather than on me and my problems. You're able to mend what's broken, even if it's my heart. You can calm fear, even in frightening circumstances. You can heal hurts, even when it's the immense wound of widowhood. And you can come alongside someone who needs a partner.

My heart may still grieve, but I'm beginning to see that I need to acknowledge the long list of good things in my everyday life—things that have always been there because *you've* always been there, unchanged. Thank you, Father. Show me how to focus less on how I'm doing and more on all you're doing.

In the name of Jesus I pray. Amen.

Now to the King eternal, immortal, invisible, the only God,

be honor and glory for ever and ever.

1 Timothy 1:17

CAN YOU HEAR ME?

On my bed I remember you;

I think of you through the watches of the night.

Psalm 63:6

DEAR FATHER,

NIGHTTIME IS HARD. I used to think that if I couldn't sleep for worrying about something, I should start praying—then the devil would *put* me to sleep. But now as a widow, when I have more to worry about than ever, that doesn't work.

As I lie there hoping sleep will come, I find myself thinking a great deal about you, Lord. Sometimes I feel like I'm being tugged in two directions—toward your truth and Satan's lies—and it feels like I might split in two. Scripture says you hold everything together, and I hope I'm personally included in that.

I really need your help to square off with this spiritual enemy. I know he wants me to be upset and will do all he can to bring me down. I'm fighting against him, but I'm not strong enough by myself. Please don't let him have his way.

> He [Jesus] is before all things,
>
> and in him all things hold together.
>
> Colossians 1:17

So why can't I get back to sleep during the night, even if I'm quoting Scripture? Could it be you want me awake? Might there be a valuable reason for my insomnia? Do you even intentionally wake me sometimes?

I've never considered that before, since I usually put sleep at the top of my nighttime list. But if you're waking me, Lord, my prayer during the night ought to be, "What do you want me to think as I lie here awake?"

There's a story in the Bible about someone else who had a sleepless night. You repeatedly woke young Samuel until he finally realized it wasn't the priest calling him but you. That's when he promised to listen to whatever you had to say.

Maybe my sleepless nights aren't as much about getting back to sleep as listening for your voice. Forgive me for using the words of Scripture like a sleeping pill, assuming my rest is more important than hearing something you might want to tell me during the night.

Lord, on Samuel's sleepless night you literally entered his room and stood nearby. You may never appear in my room that way, but I'm confident if I ask you to communicate with me, you will.

Now, with this new understanding, I'll be listening for you in the watches of my nights. I'm even eager for my next bout of sleeplessness. Thank you, Father.

In the name of Jesus I pray. Amen.

Eli [the priest] told Samuel, "Go and lie down, and if he calls you, say, 'Speak, LORD, for your servant is listening.'"

So Samuel went and lay down in his place.

The LORD came and stood there, calling as at the other times, "Samuel! Samuel!"

1 Samuel 3:9–10

ME, MYSELF, AND I

"Whoever wants to save their life will lose it,

but whoever loses their life for me will find it."

Matthew 16:25

DEAR FATHER,

THESE DAYS, AS I try to get used to life without my beloved, I'm feeling very self-absorbed. My many questions, none of which seem to have answers, all have my name in the middle of them. I'm tempted to get lost in self-pity, self-indulgence, and self-centeredness.

As I grieve, is it okay to be so completely consumed with myself like that?

Throughout your Word you encourage us to get out of ourselves and look at circumstances from other people's points of view. But my grieving experience has been quite the opposite. I'm ashamed to say I've been expecting everyone else to be looking out for my interests, even though I haven't been concerned about theirs.

How do I find the right balance, Lord? Is it possible that the more I look inward, the longer it takes to feel better? I certainly don't want my grief to stretch out any longer than it must.

I'm sure I'm not the only widow to struggle with self-centeredness, Father. Maybe the best way to move away from it is to spend time encouraging someone else who's suffering too. Stepping outside my own grief for a time might be exactly what you want me to do.

> Carry each other's burdens,
>
> and in this way you will fulfill the law of Christ.
>
> Galatians 6:2

This strategy of turning from my own sadness to someone else's seems only to sidestep the work of my grief—but maybe that's your intention. So, because it's you asking me to try it, Father, I'm willing. You'll have to show me the who and how, though. And lending a hand sounds like it'll take energy I don't have. But I know I can count on you to provide everything I'll need.

This is one of those times the Bible doesn't make complete sense to me. But then again, you and I don't always think alike. You faithfully back up your teaching in impressive ways, though, and that makes me want to try this, just to see how it works. Besides, my self-focused approach hasn't helped me very much, so I don't have much to lose in reaching out to someone else.

I want to grieve in a way that will move me into the future you have waiting for me, whatever that is. It will be a happy day when my life no longer includes this present weight of sorrow. And if I'll get there sooner by helping someone else, just point me in her direction, Father.

In the name of Jesus I pray. Amen.

We must help the weak,

remembering the words the Lord Jesus himself said:

"It is more blessed to give than to receive."

Acts 20:35

COUNTING BLESSINGS

Blessings will come on you and accompany you

if you obey the LORD your God. . . .

You will be blessed when you come in

and blessed when you go out.

Deuteronomy 28:2, 6

DEAR FATHER,

I COME TO YOU today with the hope of your blessing—because lately the burden of widowhood has felt exceptionally heavy. So I thought it would be a good time to study my current situation and ask you to define some ways you've blessed me. Would that be all right?

I know I've made progress in mourning my husband's death and should label that a positive. It would be naive to think my crying spells are over, but they do come less often and they don't last as long. That's a blessing.

Another positive is that my life is slowly regaining routine. It's different from when I was married, and I'm having to learn new ways to cope. But the return of a routine is welcome, and it's another blessing.

And I've noticed something else. Though I still feel compelled to look back to the painful days at end of my husband's life, I feel less of a need to comb through the sad details. Thank you for that. You've occasionally even surprised me by letting me look past his death to all the enjoyable years we had together. Surely that's your blessing as well.

> After you have suffered a little while,
>
> [the God of grace] will himself restore you
>
> and make you strong, firm and steadfast.
>
> 1 Peter 5:10

You, Lord, are helping me step forward in other ways, too. I'm now a veteran of grief with an understanding of what it's like to mourn a loved one. Because I've lost my husband, I can honestly put my arms around someone else who is hurting and say, "I know how you feel." That understanding came at a great cost, but I believe it's something you will use for your purposes in the future. It blesses me to know my grief will not be wasted.

I've also learned the strange truth that sorrow can coexist with slices of well-being. Humanly speaking, that makes no sense—but since I've experienced it and know it's true, the only explanation is that you're behind it, Lord. Thank you.

And, finally, because my husband has gone into eternity, I now have a much stronger focus on heaven and my eventual life there. That brings me back to where I started: to you, Father. How quickly you've answered my request to see blessings! And after all you've just shown me, the burdens of widowhood won't be as heavy anymore. Thank you.

In the name of Jesus I pray. Amen.

A heart at peace gives life to the body.

Proverbs 14:30

HURRY UP

Love the LORD your God, listen to his voice, and hold

fast to him.

For the LORD is your life.

Deuteronomy 30:20

DEAR FATHER,

SOMETIMES I WISH IT were a year from now—maybe two or three—because I can't take much more of this constant sadness. I want to get over it as fast as possible. How can I make that happen?

Some people say, "God never hurries." Is that right, Father? I can hardly relate, since the opposite is usually true for me. Faster always seems better, as long as quality isn't sacrificed for speed.

Is that the reason you're never in a hurry, Lord? Because you never sacrifice quality for speed? Perhaps, when I rush through life, I am forfeiting something important. If so, does that apply to the grieving process? But why would anyone want to linger in sorrow one minute longer than necessary?

> This is what the Sovereign LORD, the Holy One of Israel, says . . .
>
> "In quietness and trust is your strength."
>
> Isaiah 30:15

Maybe one purpose of my lengthy mourning is the many quiet hours that accompany it. I don't know if it's because I'm keeping my distance from people or they're staying away from me, but lately I've had extra time to think. Too much time, it seems.

But is that your doing, Father? If it is, what should I be thinking about during those hours? Maybe you want me to focus less on my sad self and more on you and your role in my mourning.

I know you are *enough* of everything for me. The fact is, you're more than enough. I've understood that in my head for a long while—but it might take an extended time of deep mourning for me to learn how to appropriate it.

I know you can provide enough good cheer when I'm low, enough counsel when I'm making decisions, enough energy when I'm worn thin, enough tranquility when I'm agitated, enough of everything. But spending time thinking of you in these ways isn't easy when all I want is to speed up my grief.

I know that my hurrying prohibits pondering, praying, and waiting for you to come through. Maybe, without an unhurried frame of mind, I might never be able to take advantage of the sufficiency you offer.

If that's true, I suppose I shouldn't want to rush through grief after all. If I deal with it your way, slow and steady, I might come out the other side with a fresh understanding of you. Maybe I'll even discover new ways the two of us can partner up to get me through this.

So, if my time of sorrow has to be a little longer to accomplish that, then I'm willing, Father.

In the name of Jesus I pray. Amen.

My God will meet all your needs

according to the riches of his glory in Christ Jesus.

Philippians 4:19

PART 5

COPING
with Change

FAILING AT MOURNING

You, God, are my God, earnestly I seek you;

I thirst for you, my whole being longs for you,

in a dry and parched land where there is no water.

Psalm 63:1

DEAR FATHER,

PEOPLE OFTEN ASK A widow if her period of mourning for her husband is "complete." Before I became a widow, I might have asked that, too. Now, however, such a question would make me cringe. If I was still feeling sad, it might cause me to feel I was failing at mourning.

It's bad enough that I've been unable to do many of the tasks my husband's absence has forced on me. And I'm struggling to rely on you to help me, Father. Would you please show me how to do that?

Inwardly, I long for you to revamp my life. I need a fresh perspective as I start each day, a new way to view the hours stretching ahead of me. And I need a way to mourn successfully.

Other widows would say I shouldn't focus on to-do lists or maximum efficiency right now. I should simply meditate on the fact that you love me intensely and will never let these difficult days get the best of me.

> Because your love is better than life, my lips will glorify you. . . .
>
> I will be fully satisfied as with the richest of foods.
>
> Psalm 63:3, 5

The question is, do I really believe you love me that much? Do I believe that having your love is better than life itself? That it satisfies as much as good food? As much as if I had my husband back?

The Bible tells me that "God is love." This means your love isn't based on anything I do but is anchored in who you are. So even if my mourning goes longer than usual, or if I struggle with other setbacks, I can know for sure your love isn't going to diminish. This makes me want to love you back in the same solid way, Lord.

Maybe the way to manage my new life as a widow is to stop trying to be self-sufficient. That just sets me up for more frustration. Maybe I should swap my incompetence for your competence. Coupled with your lavish love, your desire to help me will surely lessen my failures. And maybe I'll even learn there's no such thing as failing at mourning.

Father, please tutor me through these next days and months. I have a hunch that if I can just follow your directions, I'm going to learn a great deal about your all-encompassing love. No matter what else happens along the way, that sounds like success to me.

In the name of Jesus I pray. Amen.

"My grace is sufficient for you,

for my power is made perfect in weakness."

Therefore I will boast all the more gladly about my weaknesses,

so that Christ's power may rest on me.

2 Corinthians 12:9

DESPERATE FOR HELP

"There is no one like the God of Jeshurun,

who rides across the heavens to help you and on

the clouds in his majesty.

The eternal God is your refuge, and underneath

are the everlasting arms."

Deuteronomy 33:26–27

DEAR FATHER,

TODAY I'M FEELING COMPLETELY inadequate, helpless to deal with my problems. I'm encouraged to know you can be everywhere simultaneously and are never without solutions. But I've always been used to taking my troubles to my husband first. After all, I could see and hear him, and he was always willing to help.

It's a monumental shift from him to you, Father, but here I am, trying to practice a new approach to problem-solving. I realize you're far more capable at this than my husband ever could have been, but honestly, I used to trust him as much as I trusted you. And for years that worked just fine.

It's difficult to partner with someone who's invisible, Lord. When I ask *you* what to do, I feel like I'm talking into thin air, since I never receive any audible answers. Can you teach me how to bridge this gap between us? I know I need to rely on you for your wisdom—I just need to be taught how.

> "Call to me and I will answer you
>
> and tell you great and unsearchable things you do not know."
>
> Jeremiah 33:3

You clearly invite me to approach you and even promise to respond. Since I can't count on hearing you audibly, how else can I listen for you? Might it be through your written words? Come to think of it, that might be even better than if you talked to me, since I can go back and refer to Scripture again and again.

Lord, are there other advantages to asking you for help instead of asking someone I can see and hear? I can think of one more: you're available night and day, something my husband couldn't be. Oh, and another: the Bible has many practical things in it. So maybe I'll just pray out my questions to you and watch for answers in the Bible. It could be that as I work at this, you'll let me hear you more and more and help me in ways I can't now anticipate.

As a widow, I need you in unique ways—and I fall into a special category in your sight. Thank you for that reassuring thought today. Maybe it's more important that your eyes see me than that mine see you. I guess I'll continue to pray for what I need, leaving the answers up to you. Please help me to hear you well, Lord.

In the name of Jesus I pray. Amen.

The widow who is really in need and left all alone puts her hope in God and continues night and day to pray and to ask God for help.

1 Timothy 5:5

WEDDING WOES

[Jesus said,]

"Do you believe that I am able to do this?"

"Yes, Lord," they replied.

Matthew 9:28

DEAR FATHER,

BEFORE I BECAME A widow, it never occurred to me that attending a wedding by myself might be stressful. It wasn't as if I hadn't gone alone on occasion, when my husband was unavailable. But widowhood changes many things, and these days going alone is my only choice. I don't even get to chat about the event once I'm home again, because there's no one there to talk to. Now, if a wedding invitation comes in the mail, my only options are to attend as a single or stay home.

One is a lonely number, Father. When I think about it, your Son Jesus must have felt that, too. During His three years of ministry on earth, when He had the same limitations as the rest of us, He must have missed the close companionship He had with you and your Spirit before He became a man. And His loneliness for the two of you surely must have surpassed mine for my husband.

> Turn to me and be gracious to me,
>
> for I am lonely and afflicted.
>
> Relieve the troubles of my heart
>
> and free me from my anguish.
>
> Psalm 25:16–17

How did Jesus cope, Father? The next time I get a wedding invitation and have to decide whether to go or not, I wish I could make my decision the same way He did. But I'm sure Jesus was quick to set aside His own feelings. He probably decided to attend if he thought He could bless the bride and the groom and their families in some way. Sadly, I often RSVP yes or no based on what will make me the least uncomfortable.

Your Word says He attended a wedding once with His mother and the disciples. Did the celebration cause Him to think about what life might have been like if He'd been able to marry? After all, most men of His age back then were married with families. But He didn't RSVP a no to the wedding host in Cana. Jesus showed up without concern for His own emotional needs, watching instead for opportunities to serve.

That was the day He turned ordinary water into a fine wine, benefiting the host, the couple, and all the guests. I would really like to approach each wedding—and every other social event—with that same others-oriented attitude.

Would you please help me to stop fussing over how difficult something might be for me and start thinking instead of bringing joy to others? If I'm attentive to your guidance, Lord, I know you can change my mind-set from selfish to serving. And you can do that as effortlessly as Jesus turned water into wine. Please make it so, Father.

In the name of Jesus I pray. Amen.

What god is as great as our God?

You are the God who performs miracles;

you display your power among the peoples.

Psalm 77:13–14

A HEAVY LOAD

[The Lord] heals the brokenhearted
and binds up their wounds.

Psalm 147:3

DEAR FATHER,

I'VE HEARD YOU ARE the God of new beginnings, and if anyone needs one of those, it's me. Today I come with my heart aching, weighed down with woes.

I've been bent under this load of grief for a while now, mostly because I don't know how to manage my new life as a widow. My mate's departure has left a void not only inside me but around me, in little, everyday ways. Seasoned widows tell me that you'll gradually heal my broken heart, but what should I do about the practical, day-to-day problems I encounter?

My husband's absence is ever-present in my thoughts. But I face a different kind of problem when the washing machine breaks down or the checking account needs to be balanced. These and so many other chores will never "heal" on their own, and carrying them has bent me low.

My widowhood seems to demand a whole new me, someone I've never been and doubt I can ever be. Lord, I suppose it's possible you want to change me into a woman who can deal with the everyday crises my husband used to handle. The problem is, I just don't see how it can happen.

> "See, I am doing a new thing!
>
> Now it springs up; do you not perceive it?
>
> I am making a way in the wilderness
>
> and streams in the wasteland."
>
> Isaiah 43:19

I do want to grow into my new role as a single woman and live as you want me to live, if I could only figure out how. You say the only burdens I should carry are light ones, because *you* want to shoulder the heavy ones. But I need you to show me how this works. How do I share burdens with you?

You've said your burden is light. The implication is that if I link arms with you, my burden will be lighter, too. As it is, though, the load seems to get heavier every day, especially the substantial weight of my damaged emotions. Sharing that with you would be a tremendous relief, Lord. If I could learn to roll some of my burdens onto your shoulders, would I find the energy to tackle the everyday problems related to my husband's absence?

Please teach me how to take advantage of the help you offer, Father. And as we bear the burdens of my widowhood together, may the resulting lighter load bring a positive new beginning for me—both emotionally and in practical, everyday ways.

In the name of Jesus I pray. Amen.

"Come to me, all you who are weary and burdened,

and I will give you rest. . . . I am gentle and humble in heart,

and you will find rest for your souls.

For my yoke is easy and my burden is light."

Matthew 11:28–30

SEARCHING FOR HAPPINESS

Always be zealous for the fear of the LORD.

There is surely a future hope for you,

and your hope will not be cut off.

Proverbs 23:17–18

DEAR FATHER,

I'M TRYING MY BEST to accept the difficulties of widowhood, but am finding it hard to be hopeful. If I could somehow think more like you and less like me, I'd probably have a brighter outlook. The problem is that I'm always looking at life through a gauzy curtain of discouragement and uncertainty. I can't seem to push through it. Do you think I'll ever be happy again?

These thoughts drag me down, Father, and I'm worn out from pretending I feel fine. I realize no one is happy all the time, but how about *some* of the time? Am I wrong to want that? Maybe a better question is this: am I free to pursue personal happiness at all?

> It is for freedom that Christ has set us free.
>
> Galatians 5:1

Some people talk about "freedom in Christ," Father. I assume this means freedom from any kind of bondage, whether it's an internal slavery to something in the heart and mind or an external slavery to a person or situation. Since Jesus died to set me free, paying an exorbitantly high price to do so, I assume His sacrifice includes freedom from discouragement—and maybe even the freedom to go after happiness.

But if that's true, why does wanting to be happy sound so selfish? Christ's death seems far too significant to be applied to fixing my discouragement. How do I dare claim His excruciating sacrifice in relation to my mood? Is it possible that if I actually do find happiness, I'll end up feeling guilty about it anyway?

All this is very confusing, Father. What frame of mind do *you* want me have? How do I develop the right attitude about widowhood? I want to live within the promises you've given—especially those about freedom in Christ—but how? Maybe chasing after happiness is missing the point.

I would love for you to bring freedom into my life. So please start with freedom from the narrow-mindedness and wrong thinking that plague me. After that, please lead me to the freedom in Christ as you offer it in the Bible. I don't know just what that would look like, Father, and it's very possible it has nothing to do with personal happiness. But I'll bet being free in Christ is better than being happy in me.

Father, there's a great deal I don't understand. But my understanding isn't nearly as important as my openness to receiving everything you offer to give me. And whatever that is, *that's* what I want—whether it's happiness or something else. I'm leaving it all up to you.

In the name of Jesus I pray. Amen.

Give me understanding according to your word.

May my supplication come before you;

deliver me according to your promise.

Psalm 119:169–170

COMING CLOSE

Part your heavens, Lord, and come down. . . .

Reach down your hand from on high;

deliver me and rescue me.

Psalm 144:5, 7

DEAR FATHER,

THANK YOU FOR HEARING my prayers. I'm well aware you wouldn't have to listen if you didn't want to. The Bible tells me you listen to every request I make, prayed behind closed doors or even just inside my head. I know I don't deserve such a privilege, petitioning the God of the Universe, and yet you've invited me to come.

You've told me I can have a heart-to-heart conversation with you any time, day or night. Unlike the VIPs of this world, who wouldn't receive me without a longstanding appointment—if at all—you're "open for business" around the clock. This too is a wonder and something I'm deeply thankful for, since I often need you most during the night.

It's impressive that I can talk to you whenever I want. Even more impressive, though, is that you're willing to speak back to me! I don't hear you audibly, but you speak to my head and heart by way of strong impressions that I know aren't my own thoughts.

Father, I don't know what I'd do without you as I pace through widowhood. You counsel me when I'm confused and revive me when I'm depleted. You save me from self-pity and prevent me from making mistakes I would surely regret. It's because of our close conversational relationship that I know I'm going to get through the many adjustments widowhood demands.

> If God is for us, who can be against us?
>
> Romans 8:31

I love you, Lord. Sometimes it probably doesn't seem that way, since I can doubt your presence and fear my future, but beneath all my waffling is a strong loyalty to you. I'd be lost without you and don't ever want to live apart from you.

Since you're divine and I'm human, there's a massive gap between us. Your willingness to communicate with me bridges that gap, Father. And it works only because you've agreed to let me come. I'll never get over your wanting to hear from me, and I sincerely hope I'll never stop taking advantage of such a miraculous opportunity. You, Father, are awesome!

As we talk day to day, would you show me how to live in a way that blesses you? I want to be an obedient daughter who comes to you before going to anyone else, someone who's eager to follow your advice, every time. May I become better and better at hearing you accurately, because then I'll always know what to do next. With your faithful help, I know everything is going to work out fine.

In the name of Jesus I pray, Amen

"The eyes of the LORD run to and fro throughout the whole earth to show Himself strong on behalf of those whose heart is loyal to Him."

2 Chronicles 16:9 (NKJV)

PART 6

WAITING
to Heal

HOW TO HEAL

"If you . . . know how to give good gifts to your children, how much more will your Father in heaven give good gifts to those who ask him!"

Matthew 7:11

DEAR FATHER,

YOU'VE ASSURED ME I can ask for anything from you. You even tell me if I ask, you'll give. I know you're not referring only to material possessions but rather to gifts that can't be bought in a store, things like peace amidst turmoil and gratitude despite loss. So I'm going to ask you for something I want more than anything else right now: a healed heart.

Sometimes I miss my husband so much the ache swells inside. It feels as if my heart wants to burst but can't, like it has no way to relieve the pressure. I'm not even sure what the pain expresses. Maybe it isn't a longing for a husband who is gone as much as a longing for something other than the life I now have as a widow. Or maybe this mysterious longing goes even deeper.

Is it possible my heart is aching for a new relationship with you, Lord?

As I gradually accept the sad reality that my husband isn't coming home, might I have confused my desire for him with a desire for you? Is my subconscious mind ahead of the rest of me?

Because my husband is now absent, the love I still feel for him has no place to go. I thought that's what this swelling ache was all about, but maybe it's really a growing love for you instead, Lord. Now that my life-partner is unavailable, it's beginning to dawn on me that you *are* still available and that I need you more than ever.

> Heal me, LORD, and I will be healed;
>
> save me and I will be saved,
>
> for you are the one I praise.
>
> Jeremiah 17:14

Though I can't see you, I sense you're with me—and I believe the promise that you'll never leave me. Maybe if I can learn to take advantage of all you're offering me, my aching heart will be soothed.

So I'm going to be brave and just ask you: Will you be my new partner, Lord? Will you satisfy any longing I still have for my husband by increasing my longing for you and then satisfying it? Will you teach me how to praise you, even in the midst of sorrow?

I have confidence you're going to give me these gifts because you've invited me to ask, and I've taken you up on it. And as I learn to satisfy my longings by bringing them to you, surely a healed heart can't be far behind. May any tears I shed from now on be both a farewell to my husband and a welcome to you.

In the name of Jesus I pray. Amen.

[Jesus] said to her,

"Daughter, your faith has healed you.

Go in peace and be freed from your suffering."

Mark 5:34

TAKING TIME

Whatever is has already been,

and what will be has been before.

Ecclesiastes 3:15

DEAR FATHER,

IT'S STRANGE THE WAY a widow's mind works. One day I'm forward-thinking, the next looking back, unsure of where I should be. A passage from the Bible describes my dilemma perfectly. Ecclesiastes 3 lists twenty-eight elements of everyday life in a beautiful poem. It also tells me there will be a time for each one—whether to be born or to die, to plant or to uproot, to kill or to heal, and all the other experiences of life.

My question, Lord, is how do I know *when* I'm supposed to do *what*?

The list is a practical one, Lord, and I appreciate that it highlights not just the positives but the negatives, too: "a time to tear down and a time to build; a time to search and a time to give up."

As a widow, I read those verses and see myself only in the negatives, like a time to weep and a time to mourn. Would you please make sense of my confusion, Father? I wonder if you might be trying to tell me something important about this distressing time. Is it possible you're validating what I'm going through every day?

> There is a time for everything,
>
> and a season for every activity under the heavens . . .
>
> a time to weep and a time to laugh,
>
> a time to mourn and a time to dance.
>
> Ecclesiastes 3:1, 4

Maybe you're actually approving of my tears, since Ecclesiastes says we're to take time to grieve. The message I'm getting is that seasons of sadness are every bit as important as those of gladness. Realizing that has delivered gentle comfort to my hurting heart. Thank you so much, Lord.

As I live through this time of weeping and mourning, I pray you'll give me a glimpse of the happy activities you've linked with those two biblical phrases: laughing and dancing. When your specified time for grieving comes to an end, laughing and dancing might be waiting in the wings. Thank you, Lord, for this possibility. On my darkest days, it will help to keep me going.

I'm certainly not the first person to experience deep personal loss, nor am I the first to weep into my pillow or feel emotionally spent by grief. Ecclesiastes reminds me that the sadness I now know has been felt by others through the generations. But rather than being demoralized by this, it energizes me to persevere. You've convinced me that others have made it, so I know I will, too.

Best of all, Father, are the words written about you in that same chapter of the Bible—that you will make everything beautiful when the time is just right. That means when *you* say it's right, not when I do. In the meantime, please increase my patience. Help me to wait for your right time to say good-bye to weeping and mourning and hello to laughing and dancing.

In the name of Jesus I pray. Amen.

Rejoice in hope,

be patient in tribulation,

be constant in prayer.

Romans 12:12 (ESV)

A NEW HUSBAND

"I am the LORD, and there is no other;

apart from me there is no God.

I will strengthen you."

Isaiah 45:5

DEAR FATHER,

I'M THANKFUL FOR MY widowed friends. We bump into each other at church, in the neighborhood, and in cyberspace, enjoying a unique camaraderie no other group has.

Most of us share the same concerns, and as you know, our number one struggle is loneliness. That's not to say we don't have meaningful relationships with each other. Thank you, Lord, for these supportive women—but our loneliness originates with missing our men. That's something not even a good girlfriend can fix.

Father, these days I'm trying to think of *you* as my companion, someone I can be close to in a way that trumps human friendship or even a marriage relationship. Because you are the infinite God, time spent in your presence can satisfy more than just the need for a partner. It can deal with deep soul-longings, too, I'm sure. Would you please show me how to link up with you in the most meaningful way?

In the Old Testament, you referred to yourself as a husband for widows.

> "Your Maker is your husband—
>
> the LORD Almighty is his name—
>
> the Holy One of Israel is your Redeemer."
>
> Isaiah 54:5

Maybe that's strictly symbolism, or maybe it's meant just for people living in those ancient times—but I like to think it's for me, too. If you promised to be God-the-husband back then, you could promise me that today, since you never change.

So, in my loneliness for the husband you originally gave me—the husband who is now gone—my only choice is to believe you when you say you're willing to fill in for him. But how will that work? For instance, since my husband was a sounding board for me when I needed to make decisions, do you mean you'll be my sounding board now, in that same way? And since he comforted me when I was sad, are you saying you'll do the same?

Will you provide strength when I'm weak, just like he did? And plant optimism within me when the future looks bleak? And most important of all, will you let me feel loved by you as much as I felt loved by him? If you're willing to do all that as a stand-in for him, then maybe my loneliness will lift.

I wouldn't have to look to widowed friends or anyone other than you to ease my sorrow. After all, even my closest loved ones can't do for me what you can. Lord, if I could learn to depend on you as my all-in-all, that would be wonderful.

Thank you for knowing exactly what I need and for being willing to provide it for me. There's no one like you!

In the name of Jesus I pray. Amen.

> The LORD appeared . . . saying:
>
> "I have loved you with an everlasting love;
>
> I have drawn you with unfailing kindness."
>
> Jeremiah 31:3

JOY AND LAUGHTER

Laughter can conceal a heavy heart,

but when the laughter ends, the grief remains.

Proverbs 14:13 (NLT)

DEAR FATHER,

DURING THE EARLY WEEKS of widowhood, I could hardly face my new reality with all its changes. I dreaded having someone ask how I was doing, since that usually happened in a crowded church lobby or at a family gathering. When the question came, it didn't seem appropriate to answer honestly, so I'd just say, "I'm doing fine." But you knew the truth.

I used to wonder if I'd ever want to go out socially again, just for the fun of it, because nothing seemed fun. In the early stages of grieving, it took immense effort even to smile, but a smile through tears doesn't fool anybody.

As for laughing, it was out of the question. I didn't think I'd ever laugh again, and most of the time I still feel that way. The few times I have laughed were only to keep people from saying, "What's wrong?" But my heart hasn't been in it. How does an aching heart enjoy a laugh?

So, I could ask you if I'll ever laugh again—but instead I'd rather know if my heart will ever stop hurting.

> You have searched me, LORD,
>
> and you know me.
>
> Psalm 139:1

It's a big comfort to know you're aware of the turmoil inside of me. Though my loved ones are trying to understand, most of the time I feel isolated in my pain—and that's a lonely place to be. Other widows get it, but then there's the problem of me not yet wanting to go out socially with them.

I'm in a mess here, Father, and need your help. Your Word says a song sung to a heavy heart feels like vinegar in a wound, and I've felt a good deal of vinegar-sting lately. I'm not blaming anyone, since their intentions are always good, but how do I cope with sensing they'd like me to hurry up and get happy again?

I know a joyful heart can be like good medicine, but I also know I can't command my heart to be joyful. I've tried it, and it doesn't work. I'm beginning to think that you, Father, are the only source of joy in the midst of grieving. One of the benefits of being your child is your Spirit living inside me, and without doubt, He's joyful. So would it be okay if I shared with Him?

I'm not sure if joy is the foundation of laughter, but maybe your prompting of a sincere smile might lead to both. I don't want to rush your healing process for me, but I sure could do with a glimmer of true joy, right in the middle of these difficult days.

In the name of Jesus I pray. Amen.

"Blessed are you who weep now,

for you will laugh."

Luke 6:21

POSITIVE PURPOSES

I pray that out of his glorious riches

he may strengthen you with power

through his Spirit in your inner being.

Ephesians 3:16

DEAR FATHER,

I KNOW YOU HAVE SPECIFIC, positive purposes for the hours of my days. Much of my time, though, I spend wandering through a haze of sorrow, accomplishing nothing. I find myself wishing for what cannot be and wasting precious time and energy in ways that are, I'm sure, skirting your plans for me.

What do you want me to do, or not do? Say, or not say? How do you want me to live out these difficult days? Many mornings I've resolved to get something done with the hours stretching in front of me, but at the end of them, my story is usually the same: I've just chalked up one more day of sadness.

Am I even moving forward in my grieving process? Most nights when I put my head on the pillow, my last thought is that the day was a waste.

Instead of asking what I can accomplish in a day, maybe the question should be this: What do you want to accomplish, perhaps through me? Or in me? Or maybe both? Those

> LORD, you establish peace for us;
>
> all that we have accomplished you have done for us.
>
> Isaiah 26:12

questions put a whole new spin on my thinking, Father. I've realized over and over again that I can't do much on my own, so it makes perfect sense to leave the agenda up to you.

If I ask what you want me to do on any given day and then follow your lead, surely you'll supply the motivation and energy to do it. And after that, in the process, my need to be doing something positive with these days will be satisfied. It'll be something you want me to do, your purpose for me, and it's bound to feel good.

I have a hunch that when I do what you suggest, the resulting day will be well-spent, whether for me or someone else. And when my head hits the pillow that night, I might even be smiling. That day would definitely not have been wasted.

The truth is, I don't have anything to lose. Trudging through blocks of time feeling sad and sluggish hasn't helped me at all. I'm ready for something new. Maybe the best way to start each morning is to ask about your purposes for me that day, what you want to do through me or in me. Then, as opportunities pop up, I know you'll help me embrace them. And at long last, I will be connected with your positive purposes for me.

In the name of Jesus I pray. Amen.

My word that goes out from my mouth . . .

will accomplish what I desire and achieve the purpose

for which I sent it.

You will go out in joy and be led forth in peace.

Isaiah 55:11–12

A NEW SONG

You turned my wailing into dancing;

you removed my sackcloth and clothed me with joy,

that my heart may sing your praises and not be silent.

Psalm 30:11–12

DEAR FATHER,

SOME PEOPLE GO THROUGH life with a song in their hearts. Melodies bubble out of them when they aren't even thinking about it. They hum while they shop, sing in the shower, even "whistle while they work."

When my husband died, the music of my life changed. These days the only music that appeals is quiet or somber—and never am I able to sing. With my husband's passing, my life's tempo has changed, like a recording that has shifted from upbeat to unhappy.

Sunday school children love to sing a chorus called, "In My Heart There Rings a Melody." It's based on the rock-solid truth that any heart filled with your love, Father, should feel like singing. As the song says, "There never was a sweeter melody, 'tis the melody of love."

I long to be filled with joyful song, Lord, music that comes from a healed heart. I know it won't happen unless I shift my gaze from the difficulties of widowhood to the gift of your unconditional love, a love that provides refuge from suffering of all kinds. Would you please teach me a new song to go along with this new phase of life, one that has its source in you? And would you give me the ability to sing it?

> I will sing of your strength;
>
> in the morning I will sing of your love;
>
> for you are my fortress, my refuge in times of trouble.
>
> Psalm 59:16

Please prompt me daily to count the unnumbered blessings you give, since I know that even in widowhood there are many. If I focus on you as the wellspring of all music, I'm confident you'll give me a new song to sing, because your Word says so.

My plan is to partner with you, Father, relying on you for protection, direction, and every other need that comes up. Then as I center on you and your love for me, I might even find myself humming.

Please make me a woman whose inner joy in knowing you bubbles out of me. May this soul-music, then, become a sweet melody of love that even others will notice. Then I can credit you with being the one who gave me a new song, even in the midst of widowhood. I don't want to be a "merry widow," but I do long to have a singing heart. Father, may it happen according to your Word.

In the name of Jesus I pray. Amen.

I will sing a new song to you, my God . . .

I will make music to you, to the One who gives victory.

Psalm 144:9–10

PART 7

TRUSTING
in God

TRYING TO TRUST

My flesh and my heart may fail,

but God is the strength of my heart

and my portion forever.

Psalm 73:26

DEAR FATHER,

SOME MORNINGS I ALMOST can't get out of bed. Though I've had many hours of sleep, as soon as I open my eyes, fresh fatigue swamps me. The simple task of peeling off my covers seems impossible. How long do I lie there looking at the ceiling? A few minutes? Half an hour? It doesn't matter. My desire to do the next right thing comes to a standstill.

David of the Bible had a few mornings like that. He wrote of a sorrow so deep his bed was soaked in tears and his soul drenched with anguish. He repeatedly begged you, Lord, to tell him how long he'd have to endure such misery. I can relate. How long will I feel like I do?

> My soul is in deep anguish. . . . I am worn out from my groaning.
>
> All night long I flood my bed with weeping
>
> and drench my couch with tears.
>
> My eyes grow weak with sorrow.
>
> Psalm 6:3, 6–7

In your Word, Father, you don't often give end-dates to people's suffering, so I'm guessing you won't give me one, either. In David's case, I'll bet you hoped he would continue trusting you, even while he was still hurting. Maybe that's why you considered him a man after your own heart—he never put conditions on trusting you. In other words, David didn't insist you make him feel better first.

Is that what you want from me, too? If you do, you'll have to be my inspiration, Lord. You've seen how lifeless I can be under the covers in the morning, how difficult it can be for me to get my feet on the floor. Maybe I should thank you when I do eventually get up. Is that you, strengthening me to do it?

Much of the time I feel frail, like I might not succeed in getting up tomorrow. I'm longing for you to be the strength of my heart, the determination of my will—not just the will to peel the covers off and get out of bed each day but to do everything else I ought to be doing. Would you teach me how to rely on you the way David did?

Please lift me when I can't get up. Motivate me when I'm at a standstill. Remind me you are trustworthy in all you do and will follow through on every promise. You rescued David, so please, Father, rescue me from the same kind of emotional exhaustion he felt. And whenever I find myself stuck under the covers again, please empower me to get my feet on the floor. I'm trusting that you will.

In the name of Jesus I pray. Amen.

In the morning, LORD, you hear my voice;

in the morning I lay my requests before you

and wait expectantly.

Psalm 5:3

MY BOTTOM LINE

Godliness with contentment is great gain.

For we brought nothing into the world, and we can take nothing out of it.

1 Timothy 6:6–7

DEAR FATHER,

I'VE ALWAYS TRIED TO follow whatever instructions you've given me, wanting to be in the center of your will. From hard experience I've learned that jumping in front of you only results in a muddled mess.

But this time, Lord, I'm not sure *you've* done the right thing, allowing my husband to die as you did. Marriage was your idea in the first place, and we tried to do it your way. We hoped it would last many more years, but now here I am, alone and disappointed. How could this possibly be the best thing for me?

It's difficult to accept your will when it's the polar opposite of mine. I realize all my complaining isn't going to change what's already happened, but I'm having problems coming to terms with my new reality. I know my husband and I didn't "own" each other, but I'm sure that if he could have taken me with him, he would have. And if the tables had been turned, I would have done the same. We wanted to be together.

I guess whether someone lives or dies has never been up to me. That's your department, Father. So am I disrespecting you when I suggest you should have let our marriage go longer? I don't want to dishonor you, but everything is just so hard right now.

I know you promise to guide my steps and hold me close when I'm going through tough times, and you assure me I won't fall. But to be honest, losing my husband has felt like a long fall with a crash landing at the end.

> The LORD directs the steps of the godly.
>
> He delights in every detail of their lives.
>
> Though they stumble, they will never fall,
>
> for the LORD holds them by the hand.
>
> Psalm 37:23–24 (NLT)

Since you tell me I can't fall when you're holding onto me, I wonder if I might have slipped from your grip. Or maybe I haven't really fallen, no matter how broken and bruised I feel.

I know your will for me is to live a godly life, Lord, and maybe part of that is to stop fighting my widow status. Rather than fooling myself into thinking I'm holding onto you—when all I'm really doing is trying to yank you toward *my* will—I should probably just release my life to you again and again, every single day.

Though I don't like being a widow, the bottom line is that I do desire your will for my life. As hard as it is, Father, I hope you'll help me surrender to that.

In the name of Jesus I pray. Amen.

> The fear of the Lord leads to life;
>
> then one rests content, untouched by trouble.
>
> Proverbs 19:23

A REARRANGED PLAN

Oh, the depth of the riches of the wisdom and
knowledge of God!

How unsearchable his judgments, and his paths
beyond tracing out!

Romans 11:33

DEAR FATHER,

MY HUSBAND AND I worked hard on our marriage. You saw us move through some rough places and come out the other side better for it. You looked into my heart and saw how my love for him grew through the years and how each of us became comfortable with the other. And then you took him away.

I know you didn't do that just to hurt me, but it seems like as soon as we figured everything out, our marriage ended. This defies logic and jerks me between frustration and disappointment. Hard as I try, I can't think of any good reason why you couldn't have let our marriage continue for at least a few more years.

I know you do things differently than I do, and you have the advantage of a view into the future. But I have a difficult time believing this will all work out well, as you say it will.

> We know that in all things God works for the good of those who love him, who have been called according to his purpose.
>
> Romans 8:28

Here I am, though, with only a couple of choices: either I can put my trust in you or find someone else to trust.

Something inside of me says I'm going to need you in my widowhood even more than I did in my marriage, and the last thing I want is to go it alone. You've said you won't abandon me, even if I question your ways or struggle with doubt. If I'm going to trust you, I should believe that, even during those times when I feel far from you.

> "Never will I leave you; never will I forsake you."
>
> Hebrews 13:5

Would you teach me how to trust you and your plans for me rather than wanting to do things my way? Would you show me how to relinquish control to you? You've offered to help me through my troubles no matter what they are, and that's a nice offer—so I want to trust you, Father. Besides, I have nowhere else to turn.

Please show me how to depend on you day to day for everything I need. Give me the want-to, Lord. And one last thing: would you let me know when you are near? Even the tiniest glimpse of your movement in my life would encourage me greatly.

In the name of Jesus I pray. Amen.

[Jesus said]

"In this world you will have trouble.

But take heart! I have overcome the world."

John 16:33

CALM IN A CRISIS

"If you remain in me and I in you, you will bear much fruit; apart from me you can do nothing."

John 15:5

DEAR FATHER,

LOSING MY HUSBAND HAS been an ongoing crisis. Because your presence surrounds me, I know I'm supposed to remain calm as I adjust to widowhood. But this stretched-out adjustment is really getting to me.

Some people seem peaceful no matter what's happening around them, and I wonder how they do it. Those are the ones I want to be around now, since their unruffled ways seem to rub off on me. And you, Father, are that kind of Friend, too.

I know you always have calm control of things, and somehow that's a comfort to me. As I think about your Son's example of keeping a cool head no matter what, His influence begins to rub off on me, too. His life shows me how I should act when I'm hit with a dilemma and how to get a hold on inner peace even while storms rage.

I wonder if there's any way, apart from appropriating the peace of Jesus, to stay calm in a crisis. It's far easier to get upset than to remain composed, and it takes a great deal of will power to choose peace. But I'm beginning to understand that if I summon up the will, you'll deliver the power.

> Set your minds on things above,
>
> not on earthly things.
>
> For you have died, and your life is now hidden
>
> with Christ in God.
>
> Colossians 3:2–3

Sometimes I think that if I talk at length about the loss of my husband, it will make me feel better. Or if I share my stress over the many changes in my life, it'll lessen my anxiety and bring peace. The truth is that neither of those works. Focusing on the negatives hasn't helped one bit.

I long for the same supernatural calm Jesus had, and if it means I should swap complaining for quietness, then I want to try that. Your Son volunteered to share His extraordinary inner peace with those who love Him, so it must be possible to remain calm through my widowhood crisis.

The key is probably learning to disconnect my frame of mind from my circumstances and to set my thoughts "on things above" rather than things on earth. Those things above must certainly include your willingness to help me and your ability to bring serenity into my life.

I long for inner peace, Father, enough to keep me calm as I move through this crisis of widowhood. Please cause your Spirit to rule over my mind. Then, I believe, calm will come and peace will reign.

In the name of Jesus I pray. Amen.

The mind governed by the flesh is death,

but the mind governed by the Spirit is life and peace.

Romans 8:6

GOOD LIGHTING

My God turns my darkness into light.

Psalm 18:28

DEAR FATHER,

I HATE TO ADMIT IT, but sometimes I'm afraid of the dark. I never used to be scared when my husband was with me, but that's all changed now. Even though he might not have been able to fend off a robber, I knew he would try to protect me, and we would face our foes together.

Scripture is full of stories about enemies and battles. It's interesting that as valiant as the warriors might have been, victory always went to the ones *you* chose. Surely it's still that way today, even with invisible enemies like fear. You're the One who awards the victory, and I have a hunch you want me to trust you with the outcome as I battle my fears.

> Some trust in chariots and some in horses,
> but we trust in the name of the Lord our God.
> Psalm 20:7

It isn't the darkness itself I fear; it's what might be hiding in it. I know it would help if I could hand over every anxious thought to you and envision you conquering my runaway imagination. But that's really hard. Even if I could do it, I wonder if I'd still feel frightened afterwards. And if I did, would that mean I wasn't trusting you like I thought I was?

Most of my fears never come true—but they could. What would happen if I learned to fully trust you, and something bad happened after that? I guess I'd just have to believe you would equip me to cope with whatever it was.

You, Lord, are the light of my life, and I don't just mean the light of salvation. You're also the One who sheds light on frightening situations. A child who is scared of the dark can be calmed with a small night light, glowing just enough to show her there's nothing scary in her room. Father, I know you can lighten the darkness around me in that same way.

I can trust you to generate exactly the amount of light needed to quell my fears. You know whether I need gentle reassurance, like the soft shimmer of a night light, or protection from real danger, like the bright beam of a floodlight. And it's possible my fear of the dark might simply be a need for some spiritual enlightening from you, Lord. I'm learning that darkness can take many forms.

The bottom line is that I should learn to habitually remind myself that you can provide whatever light is needed to dissipate my fears. Please prompt me to turn to you right away, Lord, whenever darkness threatens me. I know you'll come and bring light along with you, and that your light will be even better than anything my husband could have supplied.

In the name of Jesus I pray. Amen.

"[The Lord] knows what lies in darkness,

and light dwells with him."

Daniel 2:22

A REASON TO SMILE

Why, my soul, are you downcast?

Why so disturbed within me?

Put your hope in God, for I will yet praise him,

my Savior and my God.

Psalm 42:5

DEAR FATHER,

SOMETIMES I CAN'T SMILE. I can't even force it. People say smiling is easier than explaining why you're *not* smiling, but that's not always true. So I come to you, wanting to explain my sadness to someone, knowing you'll listen. Not only that, I know you'll help me.

I've always known there's a difference between happiness and joy. Happiness is shallow, based on whatever's going on at the moment. Joy is a deep-down sense of well-being, unshakable by outward circumstances. Both ought to generate smiles, but since my face is completely blah, I guess I'm neither happy nor joyful. Actually, I'm miserable.

I know I belong to you, Father, and that your Spirit lives within me. Your Word tells me I should be feeling a supernatural joy because He's there, so what's my problem?

> You make known to me the path of life;
>
> you will fill me with joy in your presence.
>
> Psalm 16:11

Why can't I summon up some of your Spirit's joy? You invite me to ask for what I need, telling me I'll receive what I request *so that* I can have joy. I've experienced this joy in the past, but I just can't seem to find it now. Can you help me, Lord?

My dominant feeling is sorrow. It's hard to see beyond that, and my smileless face reflects it. Maybe the problem is that I'm focusing on my sad self rather than on something brighter or better. Maybe I need to do a 180, turning toward someone other than myself. Someone like you.

I should probably begin every day by acknowledging you, thanking you for each new morning. I should look for daily positives rather than dwelling on the widow-negatives, and I should work at practicing gratitude. Surely then life would become more joyful.

Please prompt me in those ways, Lord. None of it comes naturally, and to enjoy life again, I know I'll need to take my cues from you. Please pull me outside of myself. Interest me in the struggles of others. Show me where there's a need I can meet. And even in my darkest hour, remind me of something to be grateful for.

Most of all, rivet my attention on you and your love, your power, your presence. Once I'm newly focused on you, Lord, I have a hunch inner joy will follow. And when joy comes, a smile can't be far behind.

In the name of Jesus I pray. Amen.

I keep my eyes always on the LORD.

With him at my right hand, I will not be shaken.

Therefore my heart is glad and my tongue rejoices;

my body also will rest secure.

Psalm 16:8–9

PART 8

REMEMBERING
My Husband

A DREAM DATE

I love the LORD because he hears my voice

and my prayer for mercy.

Because he bends down to listen, I will pray as long

as I have breath!

Psalm 116:1–2 (NLT)

DEAR FATHER,

I KNOW YOU'RE WATCHING over me every minute, listening to my words and also my heart language. So today you know how much I'm missing my husband. Why is my longing for him more intense on some days than others?

Once in a while a widow will express great joy over having had a dream about her husband. She might describe the experience as a "meeting," a precious reunion no longer possible in her waking moments. She clings to her dream-visit by replaying the details over and over, treasuring this mysterious meeting.

I can't imagine how such a get-together might feel. Maybe it would be unsettling, but more than likely it would be a blessing.

Lord, would you let that happen for me? Even if it was just a few seconds looking into his face again, it would mean the world. Can I ask for that? Should I?

I know you're helping me daily, even hourly, as I adjust to widowhood, and I often feel your close presence. You're teaching me to live independently of the partner I loved, and each day takes me farther from that former way of life. But I'd still like to meet him in a dream. Would that be a backwards move?

> Show me your ways, Lord, teach me your paths.
>
> Guide me in your truth and teach me,
>
> for you are God my Savior,
>
> and my hope is in you all day long.
>
> Psalm 25:4–5

When my husband died, it was your time for him to leave his physical body, which means it was my time to become a widow. Since then, you and I have been moving together in a new direction despite my heart often wishing I could go back. It seems that meeting my husband in a dream would be heartwarming and harmless.

Maybe, though, it wouldn't be so good. It might be like going in and out of an air conditioned building on a ninety-five-degree day, adding new stress. Or it might be disappointing, filling me with waves of regret or fresh grief.

I guess the best approach is to let you decide what dreams, if any, I should have. Better than asking for a dream of my husband would be asking you to fill my mind with healthy thoughts that keep me moving forward rather than back toward a reality I know I can't have.

So I guess I'm not going to ask for a dream. If you decide to bless me with my dream date anyway, I'll know it was your idea, not mine—and your ideas are always good ones.

In the name of Jesus I pray. Amen.

> By day the LORD directs his love;
>
> at night his song is with me—
>
> a prayer to the God of my life.
>
> Psalm 42:8

COMING TO MY SENSES

God is not a God of disorder but of peace . . . .

Everything should be done in a fitting and orderly

way.

1 Corinthians 14:33, 40

DEAR FATHER,

THIS MORNING I WOKE up longing to hear my husband's laugh again. He had one of those I'm-all-in laughs I knew I'd never forget. But suddenly I couldn't remember it.

Oh, Lord, override my panic about this! I thought I'd always own the memory of every little nuance, each tip of his head, every inflection of his voice. Certainly I had memorized his scent, the feel of his skin, the taste of his kisses. But the farther my calendar travels from the day he died, the more the details are slipping away.

I don't want to forget my husband!

I know you don't want me living in the past, trying to hold on to what once was. But as the future comes into focus, the past is blurring in direct proportion to it, which is terribly upsetting.

You, Lord, are the all-seeing God. You know the history I've shared with my man, the future I face without him, and the confusion I'm experiencing living between the two. Everything is within your now-time vision. That means you will never forget his laugh or the other particulars about him. All the details—including the ones I'm forgetting—are secure with you. Somehow that's reassuring.

> The LORD watches over you . . . he will watch over your life;
>
> the Lord will watch over your coming and going
>
> both now and forevermore.
>
> Psalm 121:5, 7–8

I think the only thing to do is to come alongside you and entrust my fogging recollections to your care and keeping, much like I commit my computer work to a cyberspace cloud service. If my hard drive ever crashes, the cloud will have preserved the details. When memories of my husband "crash" and vanish, it's comforting to know you will have safeguarded each one for me.

Thinking about my married past in that context relieves some of my present anxiety. I'm sure the poignancy of my memories will continue to diminish. But maybe if I surrender my five senses to you, you'll refresh one or two recollections when my heart needs them most.

I want to adjust to widowhood in your way, Father, depending on you minute to minute. Then, when all those minutes are daisy-chained together, they'll be an organized narrative of my past, present, and future—ordered by you, not me. Whether a husband-memory is active or inactive after that will depend on what you decide to do, and I trust you completely.

In whatever way I remember my husband, though, that will never be as important as reminding myself of who *you* are and how faithfully you care for me, even in my looking back.

In the name of Jesus I pray. Amen.

> Lord, you have been our dwelling place throughout all generations. Before the mountains were born or you brought forth the whole world, from everlasting to everlasting you are God.
>
> Psalm 90:1–2

FIVE IMPORTANT WORDS

I am convinced that neither death nor life . . .

nor anything else in all creation,

will be able to separate us from the love of God.

Romans 8:38–39

DEAR FATHER,

ONCE IN A WHILE a new widow will say, "I wish I could die, too." While I still had my husband, such a statement sounded like a dramatic exaggeration, but now I get it. I have actually thought the same thing. It isn't just because I miss him. Other emotions factor in, too, feelings of abandonment, confusion, insecurity.

Without my husband, who will help me make big decisions? Who will keep me safe? Who will accompany me in old age? Who will care for me if I get sick? These kinds of questions are what make me wish I could just follow my husband into a question-free eternity.

> LORD, I know that people's lives are not their own;
>
> it is not for them to direct their steps.
>
> Jeremiah 10:23

> A person's steps are directed by the LORD.
>
> Proverbs 20:24

On my wedding day, I looked into my young groom's eyes and heard him say, "I take thee to be my wedded wife, to have and to hold from this day forward, for better or for worse, for richer or for poorer, in sickness and in health, to love and to cherish till death us do part."

But on that thrilling day, neither of us gave a thought to those last five words: "Till death us do part." It was much more fun to focus on the positive promises we made. When we strode back up the aisle as a minutes-married couple, both of us assumed our life together would include only the "for better, for richer, in health, and in love."

Now, on the other side of death's unwelcome parting, those last five words hover over my every thought. It's tempting to feel despair, Father, which then prompts a desire to follow my husband to heaven. But I know that despair and my other negative emotions are not from you. They're part of the devil's plans for me, and I don't want to cooperate with him in any way.

You've left me on this earth for a reason, Father—maybe many reasons—and I want to follow through with whatever your plans are for me. Please open my spiritual ears to be able to hear you clearly. Then, as soon as I know it's really you, my feelings of abandonment, confusion, and insecurity will surely melt away.

Father, please point me in the right direction to step into whatever future you have in mind for me. In the process I hope you'll shift my focus from those five words about death to an abundance of words that describe life in partnership with you.

In the name of Jesus I pray. Amen.

> The Lord is faithful, and he will strengthen you and protect you from the evil one.
>
> 2 Thessalonians 3:3

BETTER BY FAR

"Do not let your hearts be troubled.

You believe in God; believe also in me."

John 14:1

DEAR FATHER,

LATELY I'VE BEEN THINKING a great deal about heaven. That's probably because, when I go there in my mind, in a strange way I'm visiting my husband. As I ponder what his new life might be like, I'm certain of two things: heaven will be my address someday, too, and when it is, I'll be together with him.

Of course we won't be husband and wife then. You've made that clear in your Word. But because you're a loving Father who enjoys blessing His children, I can't help but wonder if you're going to give us a revamped relationship that will somehow be even better than what we knew on earth. That would be so like you, Lord, to bless us with something beyond our wildest dreams.

I have to confess, though, it takes determination to look forward to knowing him in a way that's now foreign to me. I would just be content to know him as I did during our partnership on earth.

Of course I can't have him in that way again. It might even turn out to be ludicrous to wish for it, once we're both in heaven, because settling for the familiar might mean missing out on the spectacular.

> Trust in the LORD with all your heart
>
> and lean not on your own understanding.
>
> Proverbs 3:5

Please give me a desire to think the way you want me to think about your heaven and my husband. I guess he's not really mine anymore, and now that I think about it, he never really was. The truth is, both of us belong to you, Father—and I know in my heart you're very capable of making good plans for us. You did on earth, and you will in heaven. There's no excuse for me thinking I know better than you do.

Please give me the will to follow your lead. You've already done the thinking and planning for me, for us. You've thoroughly considered the options and studied the future, designing our afterlives with love and perfection. The very best thinking I could ever do would never be as good as yours. So I guess I can either follow you or go off on my own. And I know which of those I want to do.

Please keep me focused on walking in your ways, Lord. I want your best for the rest of my earthly life, and even more importantly, for all of eternity.

In the name of Jesus I pray. Amen.

We have a priceless inheritance—

an inheritance that is kept in heaven for you, pure and

undefiled . . . . So be truly glad. There is wonderful joy ahead.

1 Peter 1:4, 6 (NLT)

GOD OF IDEAS

How much better to get wisdom than gold,

to get insight rather than silver!

Proverbs 16:16

DEAR FATHER,

PART OF THE FRUSTRATION of widowhood is knowing I'll never be able to do everything my husband did. Each time a task from his skill set pops up, I'm reminded again how far away he is—and how much I struggle to fill his shoes while still filling my own. How do you want me to handle these sad moments? I'm not sure what to do.

You're a God who is not stymied by any question, because you have unlimited answers. I can approach these episodes of inadequacy with a list of possible solutions, but your list will always be better than mine and will include ideas outside my realm of thought. I'd rather work with your ideas than with mine.

> We can make our own plans,
>
> but the LORD gives the right answer. . . .
>
> Commit your actions to the LORD,
>
> and your plans will succeed.
>
> Proverbs 16:1, 3 (NLT)

It's possible the best approach would be to set aside the problems my husband would have handled and immediately come to you for guidance. At first it might feel funny asking you which electrician to call or what day I ought to take the car in for service. But I'm pretty sure you'll have the answers to my every question.

Then, after that, it wouldn't be just a coincidence when a friend "happens to mention" a trustworthy electrician she's used or a neighbor asks if he can help by changing the oil in my car.

I'm beginning to understand how practical you are, Father, and how wholeheartedly you want to step in where my husband no longer can. I know you wouldn't have allowed him to die if it meant I wasn't going to be able to handle life on my own.

So, with strong confidence that your judgment is better than mine, I'm going to trust you to fill in the gaps. That way each deficiency on my part can become an exciting chance to watch you work, which will in turn build my confidence in you.

But there's one other thing, Lord. Would you plant within me a bigger picture, an ability to stay above the dilemmas of my new life by remembering your faithful provision for me as a widow? Although you can solve practical problems with excellence, I know you're also good at managing problems of the heart. Please help me not to use my husband's absence as an excuse to whine or to tell myself, "I can't." Partnered with you, the end result will always be, "I can."

In the name of Jesus I pray. Amen.

I can do everything through Christ, who gives me strength. . . .

And this same God who takes care of me

will supply all your needs from his glorious riches.

Philippians 4:13, 19 (NLT)

A NEW ASSIGNMENT

"You gave me life and showed me kindness,

and in your providence watched over my spirit."

Job 10:12

DEAR FATHER,

I DON'T WANT TO be a complainer, because I know you prefer gratitude over whining. So rather than telling you how difficult it is to get used to life without my husband, I'm going to let you know I'm trying to view my widow status in a more positive light—sort of like a new assignment from you.

I like to think that, as with any assignment, there's an affirmative purpose for it. On my better days, I might even say that widowhood could include, by your doing, some new opportunities. On my own I could never turn such a big negative into a positive, but I believe you can.

That may sound like I'm backpedaling my grief, as if I've been handed something good as a result of my husband's death, but that's not it at all. Instead it's just my attempt to be optimistic about my remaining years. And since you never abandon a life, especially not a widowed life, I know you'll bring meaning to my future.

> Rejoice before him—his name is the LORD. . . .
>
> a defender of widows, is God in his holy dwelling.
>
> Psalm 68:4–5

You are keenly attentive to the needs of widows, and your promise is to actively defend us against our enemies: fear, loneliness, and the like. I'm confident that in due time you'll teach me new ways to live productively and give me a bright perspective right in the middle of this assignment.

Now that I think about it, you already have.

Whether a husband dies after a prolonged illness or in one instant, you provide special opportunities for family and friends to express love—maybe beforehand, maybe afterwards. But people are prompted to say important things they might never say under any other circumstances. And in hindsight, I see you did some of that at the time of my husband's death. This means your difficult assignment has already included some positive benefits.

Realizing this gives me courage to look ahead into the unknown and watch for what you're going to offer. Eventually I might even be able to look back on today and thank you for the assignment of widowhood because of opportunities that came out of it.

Father, please cause me to hear your future instructions accurately, just like a student listens carefully when her professor announces a new assignment. After I've understood what you've chosen for me to do, I will trust you for the want-to and the courage to follow through on it.

In the name of Jesus I pray. Amen.

When you received the word of God . . .

you accepted it not as a human word,

but as it actually is, the word of God,

which is indeed at work in you who believe.

1 Thessalonians 2:13

PART 9

SUBMITTING
to God

BACK IN SCHOOL

I will instruct you and teach you in the way

you should go;

I will counsel you with my loving eye on you.

Psalm 32:8

DEAR FATHER,

I HAVE MUCH TO learn about being a widow. Almost everything is different from the married existence I loved so much. I feel like I need to attend a "School of Life Changes" with you as the Teacher. My class could be, "How to Succeed at Widowhood."

But with the way my mind wanders, the sad truth is that I'd be a very poor student right now. I'm like a child sitting at her desk but gazing out the classroom window in faraway thought. Please focus me on what you're trying to teach me, so you don't have to repeat the lesson again and again.

I'm sorry, Father, for knowing I need your instruction but then only half listening. I ought to be intensely focused on you and your words, learning everything you want me to know. I realize you're trying to equip me for successful widowhood—and once you do, my life can become satisfying again in new ways. But it won't happen if I don't learn from my all-wise Teacher.

I wouldn't say I'm rebelling, Lord. It's just that I'm so easily distracted these days, and I sense I'm not making any progress. That's not good.

> Teach me your ways, O Lord,
>
> that I may live according to your truth!
>
> Grant me purity of heart, so that I may honor you.
>
> Psalm 86:11 (NLT)

I'm aware that you want to take me to the "next thing," Father. It might be a worthwhile project, a changed outlook, a fresh opportunity, a new friend. It could be a challenge, a chore, a delight, or a disappointment, but at least it would be progress. And that's what I want: to take a step forward while learning from you.

Most of all I need to be taught what purpose my life is going to have now, since I'm no longer a wife. My identity has changed, but surely you do have a new purpose for me. I know you won't leave me dangling, wondering what to do with the years I have left.

Open my eyes to see your plan for me. Since my husband's death was no surprise to you, I believe you've got something special already waiting, just around the corner. My mind is open to whatever that is, Father.

Instruct me as you see fit, and I'll do my best to pay attention. But could I ask one favor?

Would you keep my mind from wandering while you're teaching me? I promise to work hard in your school. And if I do my very best, I might even become "Teacher's pet"!

In the name of Jesus I pray. Amen.

> I will praise the LORD, who counsels me;
>
> even at night my heart instructs me.
>
> I keep my eyes always on the LORD.
>
> Psalm 16:7–8

WEAK FLESH

Those who live in accordance with the Spirit

have their minds set on what the Spirit desires.

Romans 8:5

DEAR FATHER,

I KNOW YOU COULD have prevented my husband's death, yet you didn't—so I'm going to assume you can make my widowhood work. The question is, how am I supposed to deal with all the negatives?

I often think of your Son and the example He set coping with the limitations of being human. He didn't want to be blamed for sins He didn't commit, but He took them on himself anyway. He agreed with you and your plan and followed through at immense personal expense.

My situation doesn't compare to His, but I have the feeling you want me to approach widowhood with that same firm resolve. You'll just have to show me how.

If I'm figuratively kicking and screaming my way through this new life you've ordained for me, I know my relationship with you will suffer. I remember reading how Jesus submitted to your will, and I want to do that, too.

Sometimes when I come to you, though, I'm so needy I can't stop asking for things. Maybe by doing that I miss out on what you're trying to tell me. Am I not giving you time to answer my "how" questions? I do want to focus intently on you, listening for your instructions—but how do I do that while still feeling so needy?

I know you love me, Father. You didn't turn your back on me when my husband died. Actually, you probably moved closer to me than ever before. Even so, I feel like a me-first widow. So how do I change that to you-first?

> "Watch and pray so that you will not fall into temptation.
> The spirit is willing, but the flesh is weak."
>
> Mark 14:38

Right now, my spirit wants to please you, Father. I know Jesus brought you great joy with His willingness to do anything you asked. He struggled with "weak flesh" just like I do, but His spirit was always willing. And I guess that's the rub. My spirit often fights against willingness, as if I'd rather have you agree to my will than have me agree to yours.

Oh Father, please shape my thinking to be more like that of Jesus. Please give me a willing heart to live the life you've assigned to me in these days of widowhood. Give me a determination to submit to you like Jesus did rather than desiring that you submit to me.

Fortify my spirit, Lord, so that when my flesh is weak, I can still move forward in your strength.

In the name of Jesus I pray. Amen.

You . . . are not in the realm of the flesh

but are in the realm of the Spirit,

if indeed the Spirit of God lives in you.

Romans 8:9

GRIEVING INTO ABUNDANCE

[Jesus said,]

"I have come that they may have life,

and have it to the full."

John 10:10

DEAR FATHER,

I'M FINDING OUT THAT grief is full of surprises, though none of them are good. You know all things, including everything that's just ahead for me. But here I am, unable to handle the here and now, much less whatever's coming on this new path of grief. I'm not coping well as it is with the sadness that engulfs me again and again, swamping me with unexpected waves. Tears seem to come when they're least welcome.

I want to step closer to you so I can handle these confusing moments better. I must have a need to hear your words of reassurance more accurately or to follow your counsel more thoroughly, because most of the time I'm just completely befuddled.

Scripture says I can experience life to the full or, as some people say, abundantly. These days, though, I feel like my life's theme is not abundance but insufficiency. I'm surrounded by losses, starting with that of my husband.

I was happy being married and going through life as a team—we both liked it that way. Losing him has distorted every area of my life. So what do you mean when you tell me I can experience life to the full? How does that apply to a widow who dearly misses her husband?

Obviously you're not talking about the abundance of a good marriage and a happy home, because those are gone now. You must be referring to some kind of internal fullness I can't put my finger on. I do know you've promised to comfort those who grieve, and I have experienced some of that. But is that what you mean by abundance?

> "Blessed are those who mourn,
>
> for they will be comforted."
>
> Matthew 5:4

I suppose if I were mourning with no hope of comfort, despair would soon take over. So maybe your supernatural comfort could be a form of inner abundance. Does your promise to come close to the brokenhearted qualify, too? And maybe your willingness to listen to my cries? And answer when I call? Are these all part of life to the full?

Now that I think about it, focusing only on externals, as I've been doing, might be to miss some good things going on inside. It's possible you've been supplying abundance all along but that I've been so obsessed with circumstances, I've missed it. If so, I'm sorry, Lord.

Thank you for this new understanding, that when I walk by faith in you and not by what I see around me, you'll show me the abundance you're already building within me. As I'm learning of these new things, Father, I have to say that not all of grief's surprises are bad ones after all. Please open my eyes to discover much more of your life to the full, starting with the abundance you've already given me.

In the name of Jesus I pray. Amen.

> The LORD is close to the brokenhearted
>
> and saves those who are crushed in spirit.
>
> Psalm 34:18

TAUGHT BY A DOG

Jesus replied, "Anyone who loves me will obey my teaching. My Father will love them, and we will come to them and make our home with them."

John 14:23

DEAR FATHER,

I'M SO THANKFUL YOU'RE patiently teaching me how to follow you in new ways, now that I'm a widow. And I appreciate that you often use simple things to illustrate something profound . . . things like a child's giggle, or a flower, or even an old dog. I can just imagine you saying, "Consider the faithfulness of a dog toward her owner, and take a lesson." So I'll observe, Lord, in hopes of learning whatever it is you want to teach me.

The most consistent thing about a dog is his desire to be near his mistress. If she's sitting in a chair reading, he plops down at her feet. If she gets up and moves to a different room, he gets up and moves, too. And even though he might appear to be sleeping, he peeks at her periodically, making sure she's okay.

If she walks toward the coat closet, he quickly follows, hopeful he can accompany her wherever she's going. If she picks up his leash, he waits for her direction. Front door? Back door? If she gets her car keys, he points himself toward the driveway, wanting to be ready.

I think I'm getting it, Father.

A dog lives his life anchored to his owner, faithfully watching for clues as to what she wants him to do next—and that's what you want me to do with you. A dog gratefully receives whatever he's given, whether it's food or affection. And if his mistress makes a demand, whether or not he understands her reasoning, he complies, trusting her judgment.

> Live as children of light . . . and find out what pleases the Lord. . . .
> Be very careful, then, how you live.
>
> Ephesians 5:8, 10, 15

I see what you're trying to teach me, Lord. You want me to delight in you, staying alert to every move you make. You want me to watch carefully so I don't miss your cues about what to do next. You hope I will anchor my life in you and be your faithful follower.

You also want me to obey you, even if I don't understand the reasons behind your instructions. And most of all, you want me to recognize the gifts you give me and receive them with gratitude—especially your gift of love.

Oh Father, I want to be as committed to my relationship with you as a dog is to his master . . . even more so. After all, you've done more for me than any person could ever do for her pet. Please shape my thinking according to what you've shown me. And thank you for the simple object lesson I've received by way of an old dog.

In the name of Jesus I pray. Amen.

Follow God's example . . . as dearly loved children

and walk in the way of love,

just as Christ loved us and gave himself up for us.

Ephesians 5:1–2

IT'S ABOUT ME?

Christ Jesus who died—

more than that, who was raised to life—

is at the right hand of God and is . . . interceding

for us.

Romans 8:34

DEAR FATHER,

I'M VERY THANKFUL THAT when I come to you in prayer, you have already come to me. You are ever ready to hear from me, and I'm amazed at the one-on-one attention you're willing to give me.

I learn from your Word that even when I'm not actively engaged in conversation with you, you are talking *about me* with your Son. This is astounding to me, but it's exactly what Scripture says—and I'm going to believe it!

> [Jesus] is able, once and forever,
>
> to save those who come to God through him.
>
> He lives forever to intercede with God on their behalf.
>
> Hebrews 7:25 (NLT)

Father, the thought of Jesus bringing my name to you, with prayer requests He's creating on my behalf, absolutely stuns me. And if I could eavesdrop on your conversations about me, I might hear all sorts of exciting things, requests I would never even think to pray for myself.

Maybe you're discussing my widowhood and the sadness that sweeps over me from time to time, talking about specific comforts you're planning to provide. Oh, how this thought humbles me! Or you might be discussing a change in my future as I try to rearrange my life to suit my new assignment as a single woman.

Maybe you're putting together a test or challenge for me. That's a bit unnerving, but because it would be coming from you—the personification of love—it doesn't frighten me. I'm confident that if you do set up such a trial, you'll also supply the stamina and endurance I'll need to come through victoriously.

As I try to get used to life without my husband, Lord, one of my problems is feeling vulnerable. But as I learn how thoroughly you're caring for me, I can't help but feel secure. The fact that I can't hear or see you doesn't negate your watchful protection and care.

How grateful I am that your Son has bridged the gap that existed between you, Father, and me. I'm so thankful you made a way for me to have a relationship with you. This means that when Jesus comes to you on my behalf, you accept *me* because you accept *Him*. When there was absolutely no way for me to get to you, Jesus created one. My heart is overflowing with appreciation.

I will never live long enough to thank you well enough. And I look forward to thanking you in person one day. For now, let me just say that you are one awesome God!

In the name of Jesus I pray. Amen.

Though you have not seen him, you love him;

and even though you do not see him now, you believe in him

and are filled with an inexpressible and glorious joy.

1 Peter 1:8

GETTING OR GIVING?

His divine power has given us everything we need for a godly life through our knowledge of him who called us by his own glory and goodness. Through these he has given us his very great and precious promises.

2 Peter 1:3–4

DEAR FATHER,

I KNOW YOU'VE ENCOURAGED us to come to you in prayer, and to come with strong confidence. That invitation means everything to me. But here I am again, approaching with a long list of things I hope you'll do for me or give to me. Suddenly I'm feeling like a child shouting, "Gimme!"

Since my husband died, you've stuck by me just as you said you would. You've heard my weeping during the night, and you have delivered comfort. You've made sure I received cards, e-mails, and phone calls—and so many other good things—exactly when they were most needed. So I've decided to dedicate today's prayer to praising you and giving thanks, rather than rolling out a new list of requests.

> Not to us, LORD, not to us
>
> but to your name be the glory,
>
> because of your love and faithfulness.
>
> Psalm 115:1

What a magnificent God you are! You've reassured me when I've been fearful and made me aware of your presence when I've been lonely. You've brought practical solutions for my problems by way of other people who love you, too.

I'm especially grateful for the Scripture verses that show how important it is to you that widows are well cared for. That's a blessing I'm experiencing every day. Thank you, Father.

Your Word indicates that your loving kindness is delivered to me "freshly made" every morning, coming from a rich supply that has no end. I can't thank you enough for this, Lord! With my track record of failures and offenses, these gifts are completely undeserved and defy common sense. But I thank you for accepting me—despite the many times I've fallen short—and for taking care of me so tenderly, the way you have.

Father, I want to sing your praises to others in such a way that people will say, "How can you be so thankful when you have lost your husband?" That will be my chance to tell of your remarkable character and how you are faithfully bringing me through this crisis. I don't want to miss a single chance to testify to the wonder that you are, Lord.

My hope is in you, and I'm looking to you to direct my steps from here on out, knowing that if I follow your instructions, I can't make a wrong move. Thank you for offering to light my path. You are my awesome Lord!

In the name of Jesus I pray. Amen.

I say to myself,

"The LORD is my portion; therefore I will wait for him."

The LORD is good to those whose hope is in him,

to the one who seeks him.

Lamentations 3:24–25

PART 10

EMBRACING
New Life

THE WORST MOMENT

I waited patiently for the Lord;

he turned to me and heard my cry.

Psalm 40:1

DEAR FATHER,

YOU KNOW HOW WIDOWS often try to decide which moments are the most difficult in each day. Is it when our eyes open in the morning, and we re-realize our husbands are gone? Is it when we walk to the bedroom at night, ending another day without our men? Maybe it's the middle of the night when sleep won't come and each minute drags like an hour.

Lord, is there any reason for me to pinpoint the lowest moment of the day? I feel driven to do that, but it's possible such thinking only makes me feel worse. I can almost hear you saying, "Why look for the worst moment when you could be searching for the best?"

And of course you're right, Lord. What do I hope to gain by defining the saddest part of my new life as a widow? Did I want to label each low point so I can justify more self-pity? And if so, would that even help?

I'm glad you stop me. You pluck me from a slippery slope that would surely deposit me into a pool of tears at the bottom. There's a verse in the Psalms that uses the dramatic word picture of a "slimy pit," and it seems to partner perfectly with the words "slippery slope." The writer of that psalm describes how you rescued him, giving him a firm footing.

> He lifted me out of the slimy pit, out of the mud and mire;
>
> he set my feet on a rock and gave me a firm place to stand.
>
> Psalm 40:2

I need that same kind of rescue, Father.

And you did something else for the writer of that psalm. After you delivered him from his misery, you actually put a song in his heart. I take that to mean he was so delighted by your rescue that he felt like singing! Oh, how I need a new song, a fresh, positive way to look at this new life without my husband.

It seems natural to focus on how difficult things are right now, but I don't want to get stuck there. Instead I'd rather live another way, which could only be as you instruct me, Father. Please teach me to think like the psalmist, focusing on your ability to rescue rather than the misery of my loss.

Would you start that process as soon as I open my eyes each morning? I could begin by at least thanking you for another day to live—and maybe by the time I climb into bed at night, you might have even given me a new song to sing.

In the name of Jesus I pray. Amen.

[The LORD] put a new song in my mouth,

a hymn of praise to our God.

Psalm 40:3

RABBIT TRAILS

[Jesus said,] "The Helper, the Holy Spirit . . . will teach you all things and bring to your remembrance all that I have said to you."

John 14:26 (ESV)

DEAR FATHER,

WHEN MY HUSBAND DIED, his absence sent me into a swirl of confusion and insecurity. At first, my mind often wandered, surrendering to the repeated pounding of grief that smashed my thinking into small bits. I ran down endless rabbit trails, many times forgetting where I was going in the first place.

Though I thought that kind of confusion was history, now—when I least expect it—it's with me all over again. Would you help me with this, Father? It's as if the abrupt interruptions of grief have trained my brain for fits-and-starts thinking rather than a steady-as-you-go pattern.

It's no surprise to you that widowhood changed everything for me. But apparently my being a widow is part of your plan—or it wouldn't have happened. Since that's the case, I want to accept it. I love you, Lord, and know that aligning with you and your ideas is my best hope for moving forward. But still, I often don't know what to think. Would you fill in the mental gaps for me?

Maybe the key is focusing on your capabilities rather than on my shortcomings. You don't have a single deficiency or weakness in you, and you're willing to pull me close enough to benefit from that perfection. You're such a wonder, Lord, and have even offered to share your watertight wisdom with me, not just once or twice but whenever I need it. And I really need it often.

> If any of you lacks wisdom, you should ask God,
>
> who gives generously to all without finding fault,
>
> and it will be given to you.
>
> James 1:5

You don't criticize or belittle me but simply lead with excellence, hoping I'll follow. I want to follow, Lord, but you'll have to show me in a way I can understand. Would your Spirit be willing to simplify things so I can "get it" without going down more rabbit trails? Please open my understanding in new ways. Show me what to think and what not to think.

I need you to stabilize my mind, Lord. I want to be done with all rabbit-trail thinking and learn to focus intently on the things that really matter. And what really matters right now, Father, is you and your intentions for me as a widow. I can't focus on any of that unless you help me, so I'm going to count on you 100 percent.

In the name of Jesus I pray. Amen.

The unfolding of your words gives light;

it gives understanding to the simple. . . .

Turn to me and have mercy on me,

as you always do to those who love your name.

Psalm 119:130, 132

TURN UP THE LIGHT

When Jesus spoke again to the people, he said,

"I am the light of the world.

Whoever follows me will never walk in darkness,

but will have the light of life."

John 8:12

DEAR FATHER,

SOMETIMES I FEEL LIKE my life is on a dimmer switch. While my husband was with me, the light was bright—but now that he's gone, it's dim.

Dimmers have an interesting effect on us. As the dial is first turned, we notice the change and look around, wondering what's happening. But after a while, we forget the difference and find ourselves comfortable in the lower light—just as comfortable as we had been in the brighter.

Is that an appropriate metaphor for widowhood, Lord? At first my life felt like everything was darkening around me. The light my husband brought to our marriage was warm and comfortable, but without him, everything seems to have dimmed. I don't see how I can possibly adjust to this darker life.

Since I don't think my life will ever be bright again, I'm hoping you'll help me get used to the new light level.

In the Bible, Jesus calls himself "the Light of the World." I think He means that if I live my life His way—regardless of the trouble I face—I'll be able to share in His light. My point of view won't depend on what's happening around me, not even something as severe as losing a mate. Rather, I'll be able to depend on Jesus and His light.

Is it possible, Lord, that as I trust in you and your promises, you'll somehow brighten my life again? I know I can't do it alone. But getting close to the light of Christ might dispel the dimness around me. Maybe, after a while, you might even show me how to become a light myself, brightly reflecting the light of your Son. I never thought my world would be bright again, but alongside Jesus, it just might happen.

> "Let your light shine before others,
>
> that they may see your good deeds
>
> and glorify your Father in heaven."
>
> Matthew 5:16

This could even become a whole new purpose for me, Father—to become a shining light in widowhood, telling others it was *you* who helped me through. Though I've had some dark days, I'm pretty sure standing in the light of your Son would improve everything.

Please cause me to live each day without dwelling on the negatives of widowhood. Remind me not to complain or to repeatedly mention how hard it is to be alone. Teach me how to embrace Jesus as the Light of my life. I want to be someone who glows because she stays close to you. After all, you are the Light that will never dim.

In the name of Jesus I pray. Amen.

> Do everything without complaining and arguing. . . .
>
> Live clean, innocent lives as children of God,
>
> shining like bright lights.
>
> Philippians 2:14–15 (NLT)

BOOMERANG BLESSINGS

Love must be sincere. Hate what is evil;

cling to what is good. Be devoted to one another in

love. Honor one another above yourselves.

Romans 12:9–10

DEAR FATHER,

YOU'VE ENCOURAGED ME TO count my blessings (even on sad days), and you're steadily showing me where they are. But once in a while my widow-worries push thankful thinking aside, and I need your reminder to be grateful for the positives in my life. I'll probably need those prompts for a long time to come.

Thankfully, though I feel like I'm pestering you, you never get exasperated with me. Your patience never wears thin, and you don't love me less when I need you more. That's such a comfort, Father. Thank you.

Lately you've been reminding me of the many kindnesses people have shown to me since my husband died. Each person leads a busy life with a full agenda, yet they've all taken time to pray for me, send notes of encouragement, bring food, run errands, or chauffeur me around as needed. They've put me ahead of themselves, and I'm grateful.

You say it's a blessing to give to others, and I hope these givers feel blessed in their generosity toward me. Just in case they don't, though, I pray your special, custom-made blessings back on them today. Your Word promises that if someone is willing to give of themselves, you'll then give those people even more.

> "Give, and it will be given to you.
> A good measure, pressed down, shaken together
> and running over, will be poured into your lap."
>
> Luke 6:38

Today I sense you're telling me that since I've been on the receiving end of so much, it's time to start giving back. Would you show me how I can partner with you to somehow bless those who've so kindly blessed me?

I've heard the remedy for sadness is to deliberately focus on someone else's needs, turning from personal disappointment and sorrow to thinking about another person. Would you point out specific opportunities, Lord, one person at a time? Who would you like me to contact? And in what way? I'm grateful you know what would be meaningful in each case and can tip me off accordingly.

You've humbled me through all I've been given, and I look forward to your ideas of how to show gratitude in return. None of my many blessings were deserved, but all were freely given and received with gratitude. By the way, I'll bet it was you who was behind each gift in the first place. If so, thank you, Father.

In the name of Jesus I pray. Amen.

My heart, O God, is steadfast;

I will sing and make music with all my soul. . . .

For great is your love, higher than the heavens;

your faithfulness reaches to the skies.

Psalm 108:1, 4

HIGH-QUALITY HELP

Jesus came to them and said,

"All authority in heaven and on earth has been given to me."

Matthew 28:18

DEAR FATHER,

I'VE NEVER ASKED YOU why you allowed my husband to die when he did, and I'm not going to ask you now. Of course I'd like to know, but from past experience I've learned you don't usually give out that kind of information. And I know you don't have to.

You don't owe me an explanation for what you choose to do or not do, and I'm even thankful for that. It means you're a God who answers to no one, that you're at the top, over everyone and everything. I love that about you, Father.

The problem comes when my lack of information leads to frustration. How do you want me to handle that? It's a combination of disappointment and irritation, not with you but with the way things have turned out. I'm aware of the statistics that say most married women end up as widows, and I knew I probably would, too. I just didn't think it would be yet.

Since you're in command of everything, including the calendar, you had something specific in mind when you let me become a widow at this time. Although I still lean into asking why, I probably ought to stop stressing over unanswered questions and think more about you and your greatness.

> The LORD is good, a refuge in times of trouble.
>
> He cares for those who trust in him.
>
> Nahum 1:7

Because of who you are, I ought to determine I'm going to fully trust you, even if I never get the answers I want. My confidence shouldn't be in information about my husband but in you, Father, and your ability to make my widowhood turn out all right.

Scripture says you think through future plans for everyone who entrusts their lives to your care. That's me, Father. I've put my life as a widow in your hands and want to fit into whatever plans you have for me. Though my husband and I had plans of our own that will never come to be, I'm working to let go of those and lean on yours instead.

Please help me believe that the plans you have for me will be every bit as good as the ones my husband and I had. My head already knows that, but my heart is having trouble catching up.

Thank you for your patience with me as I gradually get used to my new life. You are proficient in every category: controller of time, custodian of questions, partner of widows, creator of plans, and companion of mourners. As I trust in you, I know without doubt I won't be disappointed.

In the name of Jesus I pray. Amen.

> Those who know your name trust in you,
>
> for you, LORD, have never forsaken those who seek you.
>
> Psalm 9:10

MAKING PROGRESS

The LORD is my strength and my shield;

my heart trusts in him, and he helps me.

Psalm 28:7

DEAR FATHER,

IT SEEMS LIKE YESTERDAY my husband was with me, sharing his wisdom, making me laugh, and adding depth to my life. And yet time has passed—and during that time, I've become a different person than I was back then.

When widowhood arrived, I didn't want to move away from the day my beloved died. In a strange way it made sense to mentally linger near that date on the calendar, as if by doing so I could hold on to him . . . and to who I was in relation to him. Of course that was ridiculous, but it didn't stop me from trying.

My husband's departure was so painful, it threw me into a bewildering time. But because of you, Father, I'm no longer that same, disoriented person. You've lifted my initial confusion, substituted new ways to think and act, and taught me how to live alone. I'm thankful for these things, because it helps me better manage the day-to-day demands of life.

Another change is that you've allowed me to feel again. In the beginning I was numb, unable to process the grief or even put two related thoughts together. Sorrow had anesthetized

206

me, which at the time was probably your gift. But now I'm better able to express myself, even when it's painful.

Lord, I can tell you are steadily changing me into somebody different than I was before, because the new me, the widow-me, is gradually learning the ins and outs of coping without my husband. Thank you for your patience in this process. You've never insisted I rush through grieving or aim for a specific end date. Instead you've tenderly cared for me, no matter what.

> The LORD helps the fallen
>
> and lifts those bent beneath their loads.
>
> Psalm 145:14 (NLT)

Your Word says you're a faithful Helper and a wonderful Counselor—and as I look back, I see that's been true. In the early days, when I didn't want to get out of bed, you were the One who helped me put my feet on the floor and rise to meet blessings you'd already placed in my day. You've been there from the very beginning, and I'm thankful.

Because I know you're the One who's slowly nurturing me, my hope is strong that you'll always equip me ahead of each new adjustment. But even if I find myself getting stuck again, I know you'll stand close by, gently nudging me when the time is right to inch ahead. I have full confidence in you, Father, to grow me into exactly the person I need to be—and I'm very grateful.

In the name of Jesus I pray. Amen.

> This is what the high and exalted One says—
>
> he who lives forever, whose name is holy:
>
> "I live in a high and holy place,
>
> but also with the one who is contrite and lowly in spirit,
>
> to revive the spirit of the lowly
>
> and to revive the heart of the contrite."
>
> Isaiah 57:15